TENSES ARE MY TEACHER

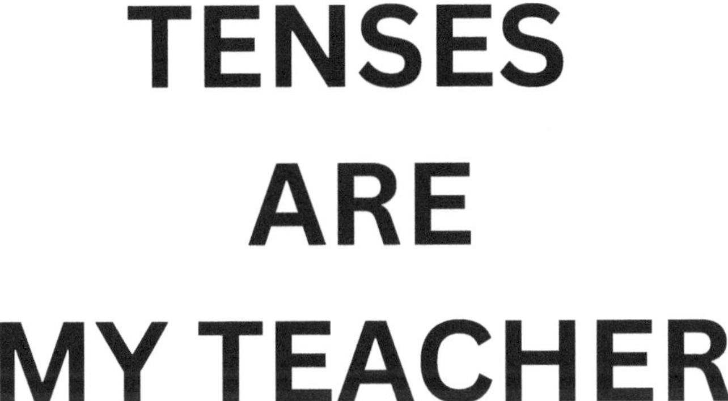

HINDI TO ENGLISH

PRACTICE PERFECT CONTINUOUS

A PRACTICE BOOK

Published in May 26, 2025

AMRITASHAAN

Name

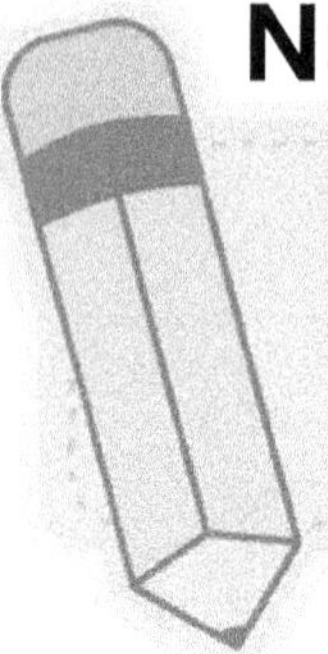

Address

Message

English Speaking

A Practice Book For English Learners

A Practice book

FOR

Present Perfect

Past Perfect

Future Perfect

Continuous

Tenses

By : **AMRITASHAAN**

MY FAMILY

Life is a voyage made possible by the care you give! The entire My Book series pays gratitude to family, and may the spirits be filled with bliss for all.

WELCOME LEARNERS !

It is delightful to see that you are at Vol. 6 and are improving your language proficiency. Through straightforward and highly effective practices, you'll further gain confidence in your English speaking abilities. Engaging in these exercises will not only familiarize you with the **'has been, have been, had been, will have been + 1st verb + ing** but also enhance your ability to use the correct verbs while conversing in English. Embrace the power of tense as your guide, turning it into your teacher to facilitate effective communication in English.

TABLE OF CONTENTS

TABLE OF CONTENTS

TABLE OF CONTENTS

TENSES ARE MY TEACHER - Vol. 6
Practice Perfect Continuous

Copyright Office Government Of India
LD-20250174010
Dated : 10/09/2025

This self-published book has undergone thorough efforts by the author to ensure the accuracy of its content. Unauthorized usage or reproduction of any part of this book is strictly prohibited without the author's written consent.

The primary goal of this book is to offer learners valuable self-practice material for self-improvement.

Disclaimer: The author has crafted this book based on personal experiences and original ideas. All materials presented are innovative practice resources. It is important to note that this book does not adhere to any prescribed syllabus, although it is highly beneficial for English language learners seeking effective self-practice materials.

About The Author

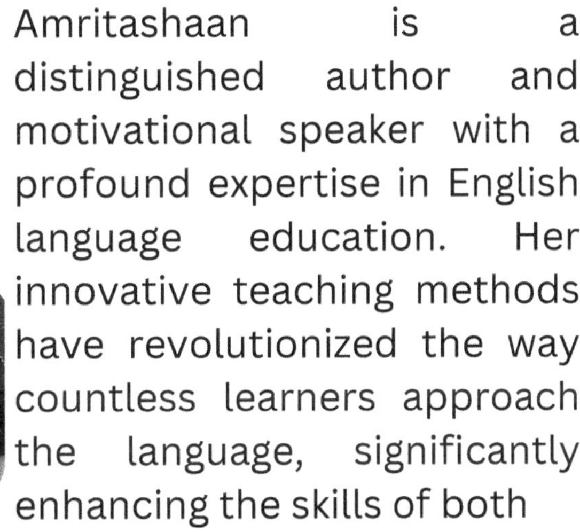

Amritashaan is a distinguished author and motivational speaker with a profound expertise in English language education. Her innovative teaching methods have revolutionized the way countless learners approach the language, significantly enhancing the skills of both native and non-native speakers. With a remarkable collection of books on mastering English, Amritashaan has solidified her reputation as a leading IELTS trainer, making substantial contributions to the field of language education. Her YouTube channel, website serve as a valuable resource, offering insightful guidance and motivation to learners. Whether through her meticulously crafted books or comprehensive practice materials, engaging with her work guarantees an extraordinary and transformative learning experience. In her hometown, she is celebrated as an exceptional educator, admired for her unwavering dedication to the advancement of language teaching.

OBJECTIVE

English has emerged as the primary means of communication for millions of people worldwide. It is employed daily to interact with friends, colleagues, and more. To actively participate in this global discourse, familiarity with English, including a grasp of its various tenses, is essential. The purpose of crafting this book is to:

- Foster a comprehensive understanding of the practical applications of English tenses.
- Facilitate independent practice for learners.
- Supply impactful materials for tangible improvement.
- Enhance proficiency in Hindi-English oral translation for effective English speaking.

Enable native learners to converse fluently in English.

PRACTICE WAY

- Tense के नियमों को ध्यान से पढ़ें।
- याद रखें कि आप जिस क्रिया को अभ्यास कर रहे हैं, वह मौलिक क्रिया होनी चाहिए।
- Hindi पाठ को धीरे-धीरे पढ़ें।
- धीरे-धीरे क्रियाओं को सोचें।
- अब Hindi संस्करण खोलें और पूरे पाठ का अनुवाद करने का प्रयास करें।
- दिए गए क्रियाओं की मदद लें।
- इसे मौखिक रूप से करें।
- अगले पृष्ठ पर अपने काम की जाँच करें।
- नियमित रूप से अभ्यास करें और आत्म-विश्वास से बोलें।

- Read the rules of Tense carefully.
- Remember the base verb you are going to practice.
- Read Hindi passage slowly.
- Think of verbs by and by.
- Now keep open Hindi version and try to translate the whole passage in English.
- Take help of given verbs.
- Do it orally.
- Check your work at next page.
- Practice and speak confidently.

Present Perfect Continuous Tense : यह काल **किसी कार्य के पिछले समय से लेकर वर्तमान तक लगातार चलने** को दर्शाता है।

1. वाक्य की संरचना - (Sentence Structure): सकारात्मक वाक्य (Affirmative Sentence): Subject + has/have + been + Verb (ing) + Object + Since/For + Time

- Singular Subject (He, She, It, Name): has
- Plural Subject (They, We, You, I): have

उदाहरण:

- वह सुबह से पढ़ाई कर रहा है।
- He has been studying since morning.
- वे दो घंटे से क्रिकेट खेल रहे हैं।
- They have been playing cricket for two hours.

2. नकारात्मक वाक्य (Negative Sentence):

Subject + has/have + not + been + Verb (ing) + Object + Since/For + Time

उदाहरण:

- वह दोपहर से नाच नहीं रही है।
- She has not been dancing since afternoon.
- हम सुबह से किताब नहीं पढ़ रहे हैं।
- We have not been reading the book since morning.

3. प्रश्नवाचक वाक्य (Interrogative Sentence):

साधारण प्रश्न (Simple Question):

Has/Have + Subject + been + Verb (ing) + Object + Since/For + Time?

उदाहरण:

- क्या वह सुबह से काम कर रहा है?
- Has he been working since morning?
- क्या तुम दो घंटे से खेल रहे हो?
- Have you been playing for two hours?

4. समय चिह्न (Time Indicators):

- Since: किसी निश्चित समय point को दर्शाने के लिए (e.g., since morning, since 2010)
- For: समय की अवधि को दर्शाने के लिए (e.g., for two hours, for a long time)

5. उपयोग (Usage):

1. किसी काम की लगातार चल रही प्रकृति को व्यक्त करने के लिए।

   Example: वह घंटों से गा रहा है।

   He has been singing for hours.

2. कार्य पिछले समय में शुरू हुआ और अभी तक जारी है।

   Example: मैं सुबह से लिख रहा हूं।

   I have been writing since morning.

मुझ से मिलो

मैं जॉय हूँ, सात साल का बच्चा हूँ, और मैं यहाँ आपकी मदद के लिए हूँ ताकि आप अंग्रेजी बोलने

का अभ्यास कर सकें। मैंने सरल Hindi में कुछ कहा है—शायद अपने बारे में या किसी अन्य विषय पर। आपका काम है इसे अंग्रेजी में बोलने

की कोशिश करना। आपको पूरा अनुवाद धीरे-धीरे मिलेगा, लेकिन उसे देखने से पहले, ईमानदारी से अनुवाद करने और ज़ोर से बोलने का अभ्यास करें।

आपका ईमानदार प्रयास आपको सफलता दिलाएगा, और आपकी सफलता आपके दिल को खुशी से भर देगी और आपके मनोबल को ऊंचा उठाएगी!

I'm Joy, a seven-year-old kid, and I'm here to help you practice speaking English. I've said something in simple

Hindi—maybe about myself or on different topics. Your job is to try to say it in English. You'll get the full translations  eventually, but before you check them, make sure to practice translating and speaking out loud with focus and sincerity.

Your sincere effort will bring you success and your success will fill your heart with joy and uplift your spirit!

Practice Time 1

- मेरी माँ सुबह से खाना बना रही है। **(has been cooking)**
- मंदिर की घंटियाँ सुबह से बज रही हैं। **(have been ringing)**
- बहस एक घंटे से चल रही है। **(has been going on)**
- पक्षी सुबह से चहचहा रहे हैं। **(have been chirping)**
- सूरज सुबह से चमक रहा है। **(has been shining)**
- मेरा दिल कई दिनों से तुम्हारे बारे में सोच रहा है। **(has been thinking about)**
- यह किताब मुझे पढ़ने के लिए प्रेरित कर रही है। **(has been inspiring)**
- यह किताब कई सालों से बिक रही है। **(has been selling)**
- घड़ी रात से ठीक समय दिखा रही है। **(has been showing)**
- बच्चे सुबह से खेल रहे हैं। **(have been playing)**
- सर्दी कई दिनों से बढ़ रही है। **(has been increasing)**
- मैं कई दिनों से अपनी अंग्रेजी सुधार रहा/रही हूं। **(have been improving)**

- My mother **has been cooking** food since morning.
- The bells in the temple **have been ringing** since morning.
- The debate **has been going on** for an hour.
- The birds **have been chirping** since morning.
- The sun **has been shining** since morning.
- My heart **has been thinking** about you for many days.
- This book **has been inspiring** me to read.
- This book **has been selling** for many years.
- The watch **has been showing** the correct time since night.
- The children **have been playing** since morning.
- The winter **has been increasing** for many days.
- I **have been improving** my English for many days.

- डॉक्टर सुबह 10 बजे से मरीजों को नहीं देख रहे हैं।

- पुजारी दोपहर 12 बजे से पूजा नहीं कर रहे हैं।

- चाँद रात 8 बजे से नहीं चमक रहा है।

- अपराधी कल रात 9 बजे से अपनी गलती नहीं स्वीकार कर रहा है।

- तापमान आज सुबह 6 बजे से नहीं बढ़ रहा है।

- उसके प्रयास पिछले तीन महीनों से सफल नहीं हो रहे हैं।

- फिल्म पिछले दो घंटों से नहीं चल रही है।

- नेता सुबह 7 बजे से जनता से बात नहीं कर रहे हैं।

- तुम्हारी योजनाएँ पिछले चार दिनों से पूरी नहीं हो रही हैं।

- मेरी सफलता पिछले एक साल से दिखाई नहीं दे रही है।

- The doctor has not been seeing patients since 10 a.m.
- The priest has not been performing the prayer since 12 p.m.
- The moon has not been shining since 8 p.m. last night.
- The culprit has not been admitting his mistake since 9 p.m. last night.
- The temperature has not been rising since 6 a.m. today.
- His efforts have not been successful for the last three months.
- The movie has not been running for the past two hours.
- The leader has not been talking to the people since 7 a.m.
- Your plans have not been working out for the last four days.
- My success has not been visible for the past year.

PRACTICE TIME 3

- क्या मैं सुबह से परीक्षा की तैयारी कर रहा/रही हूँ? (**preparing/studying**)
- क्या तुम एक घंटे से मेरा इंतज़ार कर रहे/रही हो? (**waiting**)
- क्या बच्चे पूरी शाम पार्क में खेल रहे हैं? (**playing**)
- क्या ट्रेन कुछ दिनों से कोहरे के कारण लेट चल रही है? (**running**)
- क्या शास्त्र सदियों से लोगों का मार्गदर्शन कर रहे हैं? (**guiding**)
- क्या डॉक्टर एक हफ्ते से लगातार मरीजों का इलाज कर रहे हैं? (**treating**)
- क्या सूरज भोर से तेज़ चमक रहा है? (**shining**)
- क्या इस हफ्ते मौसम बार-बार बदल रहा है? (**changing**)
- क्या पिघलती हुई मोमबत्ती दस मिनट से मेज पर मोम टपका रही है? (**dripping**)
- क्या हमारी कोशिशें 2022 से सकारात्मक परिणाम दे रही हैं? (**yielding**)
- क्या लोग एक महीने से नए कानून के खिलाफ विरोध कर रहे हैं? (**protesting**)
- क्या मैं दो महीने से नियमित अभ्यास के माध्यम से अपनी अंग्रेज़ी सुधार रहा/रही हूँ? (**improving**)

ENGLISH VERSION 3

- Have I **been studying** for the exam since morning?
- Have you **been waiting** for me for an hour?
- Have the children **been playing** in the park all evening?
- Has the train **been running** late due to fog for a few days?
- Have the scriptures **been guiding** people for centuries?
- Has the doctor **been treating** patients tirelessly for a week?
- Has the sun **been shining** brightly since dawn?
- Has the weather **been changing** frequently this week?
- Has the melting candle **been dripping** wax on the table for ten minutes?
- Have our efforts **been yielding** positive results since 2022?
- Have people **been protesting** against the new law for a month?
- Have I **been improving** my English through regular practice for two months?

- **Present Perfect Continuous**
- **Make use of 'Has / Have + been + 1st form of verb + ing'**
- **Negative sentences take 'Has / Have not +been + 1st form of verb + ing'**
- **Interrogative sentences take 'Has / Have + Subject + been + 1st form of verb + ing' + object?'**

Structure of Present Perfect Continuous Tense

Subject	Has/Have Been	Verb+ing	Object	Since/For	Time Duration
I	have been	admiring	the view	since	morning.
She	has been	applying	for jobs	for	two months.
They	have been	believing	in hard work	since	childhood.
He	has been	clicking	photos	for	an hour.
We	have been	descending	the hill	since	noon.
The lawyer	has been	defending	his client	for	three hours.
The artist	has been	enhancing	the painting	since	yesterday.
She	has been	erasing	mistakes	for	ten minutes.
Scientists	have been	eradicating	diseases	since	the 20th century.
The farmer	has been	gleaning	information	for	many years.
Joy	has been	running after	a dog	for	ten minutes.
My mother	has been	attending	the guests	since	morning.
The bells	have been	ringing	in the temple	since	morning.
The rivers	have been	flowing	with majesty	for	eternity.

Structure of Present Perfect Continuous Tense

Subject	Auxiliary Verb	Not	Been	Main Verb (V1 + ing)	Object/Time Reference
I	have	not	been	working	since morning.
You	have	not	been	studying	for two hours.
He	has	not	been	playing	football for an hour.
She	has	not	been	cooking	since noon.
It	has	not	been	raining	all day.
We	have	not	been	traveling	for three days.
They	have	not	been	watching	TV since 5 PM.
Joy	has	not	been	going to school	for two days.
The birds	have	not	been	chirping	for many days.
The children	have	not	been	playing in the street	since the beginning of their exams.
My house help	has	not	been	doing her duties properly	for a few days.

मैंने सुबह से कुछ नहीं खाया है, इसलिए मुझे बहुत भूख लग रही है। मैं पिछले दो घंटों से दोपहर के खाने का इंतज़ार कर रहा हूँ,  लेकिन यह अभी तक तैयार नहीं हुआ है। मेरा पेट लगातार गुड़गुड़ा रहा है और मैं अधीर हो रहा हूँ। मैं सुबह से सिर्फ पानी पी रहा हूँ, लेकिन अब मुझे सही खाना चाहिए। रसोई में शेफ काफी देर से खाना बना रहे हैं और स्वादिष्ट खुशबू मेरी भूख को और बढ़ा रही है।

VERBS TO HELP
Eat, feel, wait, is not, growl, get, drink, need, cook, make

I haven't eaten anything since morning, so I am feeling very hungry. I have been waiting for lunch for the past two hours, but it is still not ready. My stomach has been growling continuously and I am getting impatient. I have been drinking only water since morning, but now I need some proper food. The chef has been cooking in the kitchen for a while and the delicious aroma is making me even hungrier.

What is your daily diet and what have been taking continuously for a week?

मेरा भाई तीन महीनों से एक अच्छी नौकरी की तलाश कर रहा है, लेकिन उसे अभी तक कोई उपयुक्त नौकरी नहीं मिली है। वह विभिन्न पदों के लिए आवेदन कर रहा है और अब वह साक्षात्कार कॉल का इंतज़ार कर रहा है। बाज़ार तेजी से बदल रहा है, इसलिए कंपनियाँ भर्ती में अधिक चयनशील हो रही हैं। वह ऑनलाइन पाठ्यक्रमों के माध्यम से अपने कौशल में

सुधार कर रहा है और उसका आत्मविश्वास काफी बढ़ गया है। हमारा परिवार शुरू से ही उसका समर्थन कर रहा है और हमें विश्वास है कि उसे जल्द ही एक अच्छी नौकरी मिल जाएगी।

Look for, find, apply, wait, change, hire, improve, increase, support, believe, get

My brother has been looking for a good job for three months, but he has not found a suitable one yet. He has been applying for various positions, and now he is waiting for interview calls. The market has been changing rapidly, so companies are being more selective in hiring. He has been improving his skills through online courses and his confidence has increased significantly. Our family has been supporting him throughout and we believe he will get a great job soon.

What five changes have you been noticing in your school for last two years?

चलिए अब प्रैक्टिस के लिए तैयार हो जाइये।

आपको आगे दिए गए सभी पैराग्राफ़ को एक-एक करके पहले Hindi में पढ़ना है और साथ में उसे मौखिक रूप से इंग्लिश में बोलने की कोशिश करनी है। क्योंकि सभी पैराग्राफ़ का basic Tense, Present Perfect Continuous ही है, लेकिन जैसा कि आपने पिछले volumes में Present और Past के अन्य Tense सीख लिए हैं, तो आगे जैसे-जैसे आप 'इंग्लिश बोलो' exercise करेंगे, उनमें मिश्रित टेन्स भी हो सकते हैं। प्रैक्टिस करते-करते आप इस टेन्स को बेहतर ढंग से समझ पाएंगे और आसानी से बोल पाएंगे। प्रतिदिन एक अध्याय का अभ्यास करें और इस पुस्तक को एक महीने में पूरा करें।

इंग्लिश बोलो - 1

सोनू दो दिनों से स्कूल जा रहा है। चूंकि यह पहली बार है जब वह अपने परिवार से दूर है,  वह सुबह हंगामा करता है। उसकी माँ सुबह से उसे समझाने की कोशिश कर रही है,

लेकिन वह अभी भी रो रहा है। वह स्कूल जाने से पहले अपनी माँ का हाथ कसकर पकड़ रहा है। शिक्षक उसे लगातार आश्वस्त कर रहे हैं कि स्कूल मजेदार है, फिर भी वह खुशी-खुशी रहने से इनकार करता है। उसके माता-पिता ने उससे धैर्यपूर्वक बात की है, यह उम्मीद करते हुए कि वह जल्द ही एडजस्ट कर लेगा। सब कुछ के बावजूद, उसने पहले दिन की तुलना में थोड़ी प्रगति दिखाई है।

go, is, create, console, cry, hold, assure, refuse, speak, adjust, show

Speak English - 1

Sonu has been going to school for two days. As this is the first time he is away from his family, he creates a scene in the morning. His mother has been consoling him since morning but he is still crying. He has been holding his mother's hand tightly before leaving for school. The teacher has been assuring him that school is fun, yet he refuses to stay happily. His parents have spoken to him patiently, hoping he will adjust soon. Despite everything, he has shown a little improvement compared to the first day.

Make Sentences

Create a scene, tightly, happily, patiently, despite, improvement

सोनू पिछले एक हफ्ते से अक्षर लिखना सीख रहा है। अब, वह कुछ अक्षर सही तरीके से लिखना जानता है। वह पहले दिन से ही सुंदर लिखने का

अभ्यास कर रहा है, और उसकी लिखावट दिन-ब-दिन काफ़ी बेहतर हो रही है। उसका शिक्षक रोज़ाना उसकी नोटबुक देखता और जांचता रहा

है और यह सुनिश्चित कर रहा है कि वह कोई कसर न छोड़े। सोनू बिना किसी गलती के अपना नाम लिखना पहले ही सीख चुका है, जो उसके लिए एक उपलब्धि है। उसके माता-पिता बहुत खुश हैं क्योंकि उसने उल्लेखनीय प्रगति की है।

learn, know, practice, improve, guide, give, ensure, learn, make

Speak English - 2

Sonu has been learning how to write alphabets for a week. Now, he knows how to write a few letters correctly. He has been practicing to write beautifully since the first day and his handwriting has improved by leaps and bounds. His teacher has been guiding and checking his notebook daily for all the days and also gives him feedback, ensuring he leaves no stone unturned. Sonu has already learned to write his name without any mistakes, which is a feather in his cap. His parents are on cloud nine because he has made remarkable progress.

Make Sentences

Correctly, beautifully, leaps and bounds, feedback, leave no stone unturned, a feather in one's cap

जॉय और उसके दोस्त उत्साहित महसूस कर रहे हैं क्योंकि वे कई दिनों से वृक्षारोपण दिवस का इंतजार कर रहे थे। वह पल आखिरकार आ गया है और वे बड़े उत्साह के साथ पौधे लगा रहे हैं। वे पौधों को सावधानीपूर्वक पानी देते आ रहे हैं और यह सुनिश्चित कर रहे हैं कि प्रत्येक पौधा मजबूती से मिट्टी में लगाया गया हो। उनके शिक्षक हमेशा उन्हें प्रकृति की देखभाल करने के लिए प्रेरित करते आए हैं और आज, वे उस सीख को अमल में ला रहे हैं। जैसे-जैसे वे मिलकर काम करते हैं, उन्हें एहसास होता है कि छोटे प्रयास लंबे समय में फल देते हैं।

feel, wait, arrive, plant, water, ensure, place, encouraged, put, work, realize, bear

Speak English - 3

Joy and his friends are feeling excited as they have been waiting for Tree Plantation Day for many days. The moment has finally arrived, and they are planting saplings with great enthusiasm. They have been watering the plants carefully and ensuring each one has been placed firmly in the soil. Their teachers have always encouraged them to care for nature and today, they are putting that lesson into action. As they work together, they realize that small efforts bear fruit in the long run.

Make Sentences

Feel excited, enthusiasm, carefully, firmly, put a lesson into action, small efforts bear fruit, in the long run

जॉय पिछले एक हफ्ते से बुखार से पीड़ित है, और वह कुछ दिनों से स्कूल नहीं जा रहा है। उसके डॉक्टर ने उसे आराम करने और अधिक मेहनत से बचने की सलाह दी है, इसलिए वह इन निर्देशों का

सावधानीपूर्वक पालन कर रहा है। वायरल बुखार पिछले एक महीने से जंगल की आग की तरह फैल रहा है और कई बच्चे इसकी चपेट में आ चुके हैं। हालांकि वह अपनी कक्षा से अनुपस्थित हो रहा है, लेकिन वह जानता है कि स्वास्थ्य पहले आता है, और वह जल्द ही फिर से ठीक हो जाएगा।

suffer, go, advised, avoid, follow, spread, fall, miss, know, come, bounce back

Speak English - 4

Joy has been suffering from fever for a week, and he has not been going to school for a few days. His doctor has advised him to take rest and avoid exertion, so he has been following the instructions carefully. The viral fever has been spreading like wildfire for a month and many children have fallen prey to it. Though he been missing his classes, he knows that health comes first and he will bounce back soon.

Make Sentences

Exertion, instruction, carefully, like wild fire, fallen prey, though, bounce back

इंग्लिश बोलो - 5

जॉय, जो थोड़ा भुलक्कड़ है, सुबह से अपनी घर की चाबी खोज रहा है। उसने घर के हर कोने को देख लिया है, लेकिन ऐसा लगता है कि वह हवा में गायब हो गई है। उसकी माँ भी उसकी मदद कर रही है, लेकिन कहीं कोई सुराग नहीं मिल रहा। सभी उस पर चिल्ला रहे हैं और उसे ध्यान केंद्रित करने और सोचने के लिए कह रहे हैं कि चाबी कहाँ हो सकती है। जैसे ही वह हार मानने वाला होता है, उसे अपनी जेब में चाबी मिल जाती है, और सभी ज़ोर से हंस पड़ते हैं।

Speak English - 5

Joy who is a little absent minded, has been searching for his house key since morning. He has checked every corner of the house but it seems to have vanished into thin air. His mother has been helping him to look for it but there is no clue. Every one is yelling at him and asking him to concentrate and think where it could be. Just as he is about to give up, he finds it in his pocket, and everyone bursts into laughter.

Make Sentences

Absent minded, vanish in thin air, to give up, burst into laughter

जॉय तीन दिनों से एक विज्ञान प्रदर्शनी में भाग ले रहे हैं और उन्होंने रोमांचक तथ्य सीखे हैं। वह ज्ञान को स्पंज की तरह सोख रहे हैं और विशेषज्ञों से मिल रहे हैं, जो क्रांतिकारी आविष्कारों पर प्रकाश डाल रहे हैं। हर सत्र नए दरवाजे खोल रहा है और वह लगन से नोट्स ले रहे हैं। एक रोबोटिक्स प्रोजेक्ट पहले दिन से ही सबका ध्यान खींच रहा है। यह दिखा रहा है कि artificial intelligence कैसे रोजमर्रा की जिंदगी में क्रांति ला रहा है और दर्शक इसे दिल थामकर देख रहे हैं। प्रदर्शनी में

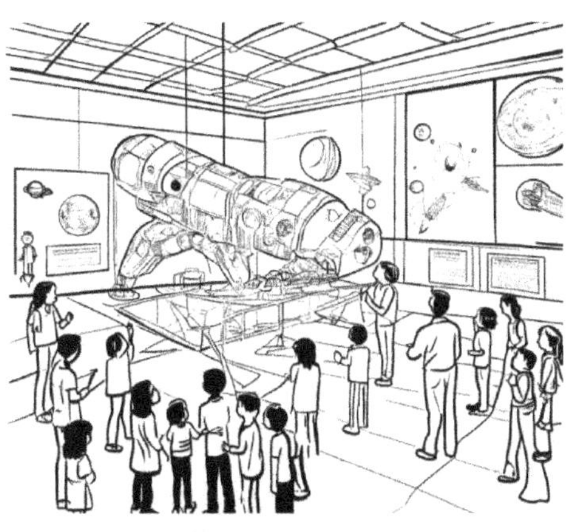

उत्साह चरम पर है और जॉय हर विवरण को समझने में कोई कसर नहीं छोड़ रहे हैं। उनकी जिज्ञासा बढ़ रही है और वह इस सुनहरे अवसर का पूरा लाभ उठा रहा है।

attend, learn, soaking up, open. keep taking, catch, demonstrate, revolutionize, watch, buzz, grow, making

Joy has been attending a science exhibition for three days and has learned fascinating facts. He is soaking up knowledge like a sponge and is meeting experts who are shedding light on groundbreaking inventions. Every session is opening new doors and he keeps taking notes diligently. A robotics project has been catching every eye since the first day. It has been demonstrating how artificial intelligence is revolutionizing daily life and visitors are watching it with bated breath. The exhibition has been buzzing with excitement and Joy is leaving no stone unturned to grasp every detail. His curiosity is growing and he is making the most of this golden opportunity.

> **Describe a science project you have been working on for a few days.**

जॉय एक हफ्ते से भाषा सीखने की कार्यशाला में भाग ले रहा है और वह मेहनत से अभ्यास कर रहा है। हालांकि, वह बार-बार अटपटे शब्दों का प्रयोग करके अपनी ही टांग पर कुल्हाड़ी मार रहा है।

वह "She has go" कह रहा है बजाय "She has gone" के और **articles** भूल रहा है, जिससे उसके वाक्य अजीब लगते हैं। वह हमेशा

"I am understand" कहता है, जबकि सही "I understand" है। हालांकि वह सुधार कर रहा है, लेकिन उसकी मज़ेदार गलतियाँ सभी को हंसी से लोटपोट कर देती हैं!

has forgotten, left, sneak out, seems, bitten off, look, has been running, smiled

Speak English - 7

Joy has been attending a language learning workshop for a  week, and he has been practicing diligently. However, he keeps putting his foot in his mouth by mixing up words. He is saying "She has go" instead of "She has gone," and he has been forgetting articles, making sentences sound odd. He always says "I am understand" instead of "I understand." Though he has been improving, his silly mistakes still keep everyone in stitches!

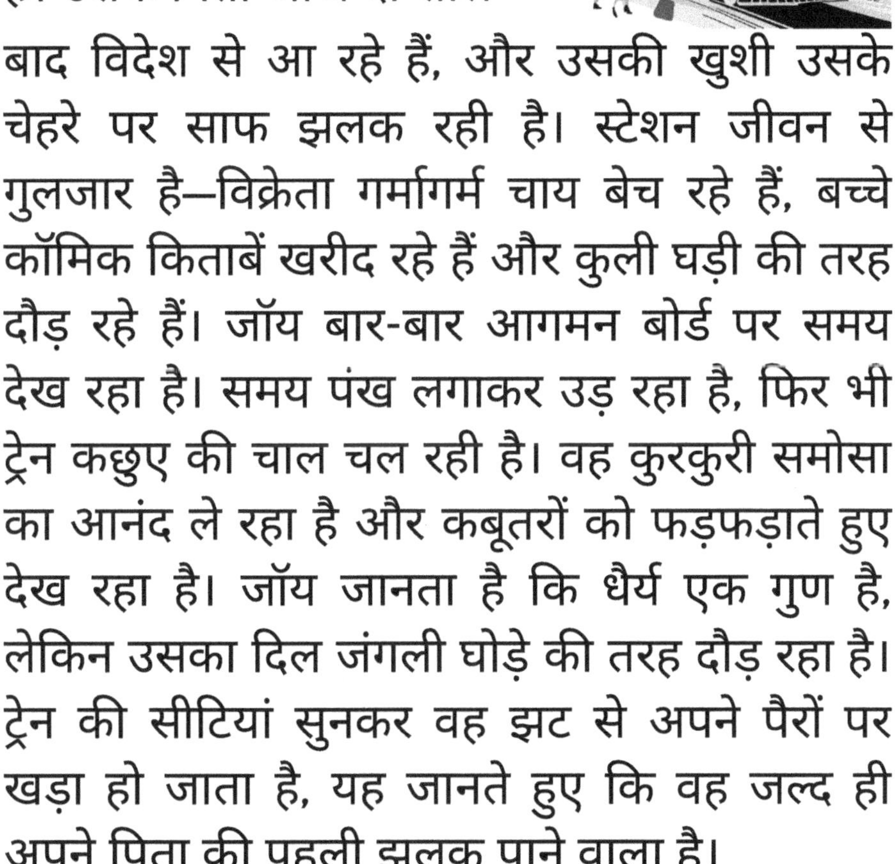

जॉय अपने शहर के रेलवे स्टेशन पर पिछले आधे घंटे से सुपर एक्सप्रेस ट्रेन का इंतजार कर रहा है। उसके पिता आज दो साल बाद विदेश से आ रहे हैं, और उसकी खुशी उसके चेहरे पर साफ झलक रही है। स्टेशन जीवन से गुलजार है—विक्रेता गर्मागर्म चाय बेच रहे हैं, बच्चे कॉमिक किताबें खरीद रहे हैं और कुली घड़ी की तरह दौड़ रहे हैं। जॉय बार-बार आगमन बोर्ड पर समय देख रहा है। समय पंख लगाकर उड़ रहा है, फिर भी ट्रेन कछुए की चाल चल रही है। वह कुरकुरी समोसा का आनंद ले रहा है और कबूतरों को फड़फड़ाते हुए देख रहा है। जॉय जानता है कि धैर्य एक गुण है, लेकिन उसका दिल जंगली घोड़े की तरह दौड़ रहा है। ट्रेन की सीटियां सुनकर वह झट से अपने पैरों पर खड़ा हो जाता है, यह जानते हुए कि वह जल्द ही अपने पिता की पहली झलक पाने वाला है।

has told, little did he know, backfired, missed, happened to meet, jumping, realized, hit

Speak English - 8

Joy has been waiting for the Super Express Train at the railway station of his town for half an hour. His father is coming from abroad today after two years, and excitement is written all over his face. The station is bustling with life—vendors are selling piping hot tea, children are buying comic books and porters are running like clockwork. Joy has been checking time at the arrival board again and again. Time is flying, yet the train is dragging its feet. He has been savoring a crispy samosa, watching pigeons fluttering around. Joy knows patience is a virtue but his heart has been racing like a wild horse. The whistling train makes him jump to his feet, knowing he will soon catch the first glimpse of his father.

Fib has backfired, missed the boat, regret has hit him like a ton of bricks

स्थानीय सरकार सराहना की पात्र है क्योंकि वह पिछले कुछ वर्षों से महत्वपूर्ण सामाजिक विकास परियोजनाओं को लागू कर रही है। वह पहले दिन से ही कम आय वाले परिवारों के लिए किफायती आवास का निर्माण कर रही है। अधिकारी पिछले दो वर्षों से सार्वजनिक परिवहन को अपग्रेड कर रहे हैं ताकि निर्बाध कनेक्टिविटी सुनिश्चित की जा सके। अधिकारी पिछले एक वर्ष से सभी को बेहतर चिकित्सा सेवाएं प्रदान करने के लिए स्वास्थ्य देखभाल बुनियादी ढांचे को सुदृढ़ कर रहे हैं। इसके अलावा, शिक्षा क्षेत्र में लगातार सुधार हो रहा है ताकि सीखने के स्तर को ऊंचा किया जा सके, जिससे वर्तमान students को अधिक लाभ मिल रहा है।

have heard, told, have been chosen, believe, hit, reminded, contribute, promised, believes, pull off

Speak English - 9

The local government deserves applause as it has been implementing significant societal development projects for the last few years. It has been constructing affordable housing to accommodate low-income families since day one. Authorities have been upgrading public transportation for two years to ensure seamless connectivity. Officials have been enhancing healthcare infrastructure for a year to provide better medical services to all. Moreover, the education sector has been undergoing continuous reforms to elevate learning standards, proving more lucrative for present learners.

Make Sentences

Hit the jackpot, Pull something off, Flying colors

संगम पर आध्यात्मिक गतिविधियों का दिव्य दृश्य शुद्ध धार्मिकता के सार को प्रकट कर रहा है। श्रद्धालु महाकुंभ के प्रारंभ से ही प्रयागराज आ रहे हैं और

पवित्र अनुष्ठानों में लीन हो रहे हैं। वे अपने पापों के प्रायश्चित के लिए पवित्र संगम में स्नान कर रहे हैं। पुजारी वैदिक मंत्रों का जाप कर रहे हैं, जिससे एक दिव्य वातावरण बन रहा है। तीर्थयात्री प्रार्थनाएँ कर रहे हैं और नदी के किनारे दीप प्रज्वलित कर रहे हैं। कई लोग दान-पुण्य में संलग्न हैं, जरूरतमंदों को भोजन और आवश्यक वस्तुएं वितरित कर रहे हैं और सच्ची भक्ति की भावना को अपनाते जा रहे हैं।

got tired, completed, moved, prepared, cleaned, carried, felt, left, feels the need, realized

Speak English - 10

The divine sight of spiritual activities at Sangam reveals the essence of pure religiosity.

Devotees have been flocking to Prayagraj since the beginning of Maha Kumbh, immersing themselves in sacred rituals. They have been taking holy dips in the sacred Sangam to cleanse their sins. Priests have been chanting Vedic hymns, creating a divine atmosphere. Pilgrims have been offering prayers and lighting oil lamps along the riverbanks. Many have been engaging in charity, distributing food and essentials to the needy, embracing the true spirit of devotion.

MAKE SENTENCES
Feel like the last straw, to catch the breath

अतिथियों का स्वागत हाथ जोड़कर 'नमस्ते' कहने की संस्कृति हमारे देश में सदियों से गहरी जड़ें जमा चुकी है। यह सम्मान, विनम्रता और आत्मीयता का प्रतीक रही है।

लोग कृतज्ञता और शुभेच्छा व्यक्त करने के लिए इस परंपरा का पालन करते आ रहे हैं। यह परंपरा एकता को बढ़ावा दे रही है और सकारात्मक ऊर्जा फैला रही है। यहां तक कि भारतीय प्रसिद्ध हस्तियां भी हाथ मिलाने के बजाय 'नमस्ते' कहकर अभिवादन कर रही हैं और उन्हें उसी प्रकार प्रत्युत्तर भी मिलता है। आज यह भाव हमारी सांस्कृतिक शान बन चुका है और इसे वैश्विक स्तर पर स्वीकार किया गया है।

rooted, symbolizing, following, fostering, spreading, greeting, become, accepted

Speak English - 11

The culture of greeting guests with folded hands and saying 'Namaste' has been deeply rooted in our country for centuries. It has been symbolizing respect, humility, and warmth. People have been following this practice to express gratitude and goodwill. This tradition has been fostering unity and spreading positive energy. Even Indian celebrities, instead of shaking hands, have been greeting others with 'Namaste' and are reciprocated in the same way. This gesture today has become our cultural pride and it has been globally accepted.

इंग्लिश बोलो - 12

जैसे ही वसंत ऋतु आती है, मधुमक्खियाँ अपने छत्तों में मीठा शहद भरना शुरू कर देती हैं। उनका जीवन हमेशा से कड़ी मेहनत और अनुशासन से

जुड़ा रहा है। मधुमक्खियाँ फूलों से रस इकट्ठा करके लगातार शहद बना रही हैं। वे अपने छत्तों को बड़े ध्यान से बना और संभाल रही हैं। हर मधुमक्खी अपना काम अच्छे से कर रही है, चाहे वह श्रमिक हो,

नर हो या रानी। लगातार काम में लगे रहने के कारण ही उन्हें 'व्यस्त मधुमक्खी' कहा जाता है। उन्होंने हमेशा इंसानों को मेहनती और लगनशील बने रहने की प्रेरणा दी है।

As the spring season arrives, honeybees have started filling their hives with sweet honey. Their life has been revolving around hard work and discipline for ages. Honeybees have been collecting nectar from flowers and producing honey tirelessly. They have been building and maintaining their hives with great precision. Each bee has been performing its role efficiently, whether as a worker, a drone, or a queen. Due to their constant activity, honeybees have been called 'busy bees.' They have always inspired humans to remain diligent and persistent in their endeavors.

Practice Exercise

- **Fill in the blanks as directed. .**
  - She ____ **(write)** a novel for the past six months. (Present Perfect Continuous)
  - The sun ____ **(rise)** in the east. (Present Indefinite)
  - They ____ **(complete)** their project just now. (Present Perfect)
  - The children ____ **(play)** in the park every evening. (Present Indefinite)
  - He ____ **(wait)** for the bus since morning. (Present Perfect Continuous)
  - We ____ **(attend)** this seminar right now. (Present Continuous)
  - She ____ never ____ **(visit)** the Taj Mahal. (Present Perfect)
  - The teacher ____ **(explain)** the concept at the moment. (Present Continuous)
  - My parents ____ **(live)** in this city for ten years. (Present Perfect Continuous)
  - The train ____ **(arrive)** at the station. (Present Perfect)
  - The students ____ **(discuss)** the topic for an hour. (Present Perfect Continuous)
  - He usually ____ **(wake)** up early in the morning. (Present Indefinite)

Practice Answer

1. She **has been writing** a novel for the past six months.
2. The sun **rises** in the east.
3. They **have completed** their project just now.
4. The children **play** in the park every evening.
5. He **has been waiting** for the bus since morning.
6. We **are attending** this seminar right now.
7. She **has never visited** the Taj Mahal.
8. The teacher **is explaining** the concept at the moment.
9. My parents **have been living** in this city for ten years.
10. The train **has arrived** at the station.
11. The students **have been discussing** the topic for an hour.
12. He usually **wakes up** early in the morning.

Instructions: Each sentence contains **an error**. Identify the mistake and rewrite the sentence correctly.

- She goes to the market yesterday.
- I am seeing him last week.
- He will go to school when he was five.
- By the time you reached, I completed my work.
- They was playing football when I arrived.
- She has written the letter before you called her.
- The sun rises when we were on the way.
- We are watching a movie last night.
- He did not came to the party.
- I am living in Delhi since five years.
- She reads a book when the lights went off.
- By next year, he is finishing his course.

Practice Answer

Correct Answers:

- She **went** to the market yesterday.
- I **saw** him last week.
- He **went** to school when he was five.
- By the time you reached, I **had completed** my work.
- They **were playing** football when I arrived.
- She **had written** the letter before you called her.
- The sun **was rising** when we were on the way.
- We **watched** a movie last night.
- He **did not come** to the party.
- I **have been living** in Delhi for five years.
- She **was reading** a book when the lights went off.
- By next year, he **will have finished** his course.

- बच्चे अपने कमरों में सो रहे हैं लेकिन उनकी मां सुबह से ही घर के काम निपटा रही हैं।

- पिता जी अभी पेपर पढ़ रहे हैं लेकिन दादी मां सुबह से रामायण का पाठ कर रही हैं।

- मैं अपने दोस्त से बात कर रहा हूँ जबकि मेरा छोटा भाई दो घंटे से गेम खेल रहा है।

- पड़ोसी अपने बगीचे में पानी डाल रहे हैं, लेकिन उनकी बेटी दोपहर से सो रही है।

- हमारे शिक्षक क्लास में पढ़ा रहे हैं, लेकिन हम सुबह से नोट्स बना रहे हैं।

- सुरेश मोबाइल चला रहा है, जबकि उसकी बहन सुबह से घर की सफाई कर रही है।

- मैं अब काम कर रहा हूँ लेकिन मेरा कंप्यूटर एक घंटे से अपडेट हो रहा है।

- कुत्ता दरवाजे पर भौंक रहा है लेकिन बिल्ली सुबह से रसोई में छुपी हुई है।

- हमारी टीम अभी मैच खेल रही है लेकिन कोच सुबह से खिलाड़ियों को निर्देश दे रहे हैं।

- वे पार्क में टहल रहे हैं जबकि उनके दादा जी सुबह से अखबार पढ़ रहे हैं।

- तुम गाना गा रहे हो, पर तुम्हारी बहन काफी देर से गिटार बजा रही है।

- डॉक्टर मरीज की जांच कर रहे हैं लेकिन नर्स सुबह से दवाइयाँ बाँट रही है।

Practice Time

- शिक्षक ने जॉय को दंडित किया है क्योंकि वह लंबे समय से कक्षा में व्यवधान उत्पन्न कर रहा है।
- डॉक्टर ने मरीज को आराम करने की सलाह दी है, वह कई दिनों से सिरदर्द की शिकायत कर रहा है।
- पुलिस ने उस युवक को गिरफ्तार किया है क्योंकि वह महीनों से संदिग्ध गतिविधियों में शामिल रहा है।
- माँ ने बेटे को डाँटा है, वह घंटों से मोबाइल चला रहा है।
- Principal ने घोषणा की है क्योंकि छात्र पिछले कई दिनों से अनुशासनहीनता दिखा रहे हैं।
- कर्मचारी ने इस्तीफा दे दिया है क्योंकि वह लंबे समय से ओवरटाइम कर रहा है।
- रामू ने नया फोन खरीदा है क्योंकि वह बहुत समय से पुराने फोन का उपयोग कर रहा है।
- मैंने तुम्हारा इंतज़ार खत्म कर दिया है क्योंकि तुम सुबह से समय पर नहीं आ रहे हो।
- सरकार ने बिजली शुल्क बढ़ा दिया है क्योंकि पिछले कुछ महीनों से खपत लगातार बढ़ रही है।
- शिखा ने अपनी नौकरी छोड़ दी है क्योंकि वह वर्षों से मानसिक दबाव में काम कर रही है।
- शिक्षक ने छात्र को पुरस्कार दिया है क्योंकि वह लगातार मेहनत कर रहा है।
- अदालत ने सजा सुनाई है क्योंकि आरोपी लंबे समय से अपराधों में संलिप्त रहा है।

Practice Time

- बच्चे दस दिनों से अपनी छुट्टियों का आनंद ले रहे हैं, वे अपनी छुट्टियों के दौरान पिकनिक स्थलों पर जाते हैं।
- वह सुबह से गाना गा रही है, वह रोज़ नए गानों की प्रैक्टिस करती है।
- मैं कई दिनों से इस किताब को पढ़ रहा हूँ, मैं हर दिन कुछ नए पन्ने पढ़ता हूँ।
- वे कई सालों से गाँव में रह रहे हैं, वे हर शाम मंदिर जाते हैं।
- शिक्षक घंटों से ऑनलाइन पढ़ा रहे हैं, वे छात्रों से प्रश्न पूछते हैं।
- माँ सुबह से रसोई में काम कर रही हैं, वे हर दिन स्वादिष्ट खाना बनाती हैं।
- पापा हफ्तों से अपनी रिपोर्ट पर काम कर रहे हैं, वे हर दिन समय पर ऑफिस जाते हैं।
- रीमा घंटों से नाच रही है, वह हर शनिवार को नृत्य कक्षा में जाती है।
- हम सुबह से कमरे की सफाई कर रहे हैं, हम हर रविवार को सफाई करते हैं।
- वे दोपहर से एक-दूसरे से बात कर रहे हैं, वे रोज़ स्कूल में मिलते हैं।
- बच्ची शाम से चित्र बना रही है, वह रोज़ कुछ नया बनाना पसंद करती है।
- चिड़िया सुबह से चहचहा रही है, वह रोज़ आँगन में आती है।

Practice Time

- जॉय दो साल से किसी खेल प्रतियोगिता में हिस्सा नहीं ले रहे थे लेकिन इस बार वह हॉकी टीम में शामिल होगा।

- रीना कई दिनों से ऑफिस देर से आ रही है लेकिन अब वह समय पर पहुँचेगी।

- बच्चे सुबह से पढ़ाई कर रहे हैं लेकिन शाम को वे पार्क में खेलेंगे।

- हम कई महीनों से नई किताब की योजना बना रहे हैं लेकिन अब हम उसे प्रकाशित करेंगे।

- माँ सुबह से खाना बना रही हैं लेकिन रात का खाना पिताजी बनाएंगे।

- तुम कई दिनों से मुझसे बात नहीं कर रहे हो लेकिन कल हम मिलकर बैठेंगे।

- यह कंपनी पिछले तीन सालों से नुकसान झेल रही है लेकिन अब यह मुनाफ़ा कमाएगी।

- शिक्षक कई हफ्तों से ऑनलाइन क्लास ले रहे हैं लेकिन अगली बार वह स्कूल आएंगे।

- मैं काफी समय से गिटार सीख रहा हूँ लेकिन अगले महीने मैं स्टेज पर परफॉर्म करूंगा।

- वे दोपहर से बारिश का इंतज़ार कर रहे हैं लेकिन रात तक बारिश होगी।

- पुलिस कई दिनों से उस चोर की तलाश कर रही थी लेकिन अब वे उसे पकड़ेंगे।

- हम बहुत समय से इस फिल्म का ट्रेलर देखना चाह रहे थे लेकिन अब हम पूरी फिल्म देखेंगे।

Describe The picture and Answer The Given Questions

1. What does Joy do every day? Why?
2. What did Joy do yesterday? Why?
3. What is Joy doing right now and why?
4. Who will Joy visit tomorrow and why?

Describe The picture and Answer The Given Questions

Write one story in 100 words either on the sparrow or on the cat, the rabbits or on the dog.

Describe The picture and Answer The Given Questions

1. What has the woman been doing in the kitchen?
2. How long has the girl been studying at the table?
3. What has the man been fixing in the garage?
4. Why do you think the dog has been barking near the door?
5. Where has the cat been resting and for how long?

Look at the Pictures and Write a Story

Write a story on this picture in 100 words

Make Your Notes

Make Your Notes

Make Your Notes

Make Your Notes

LET'S
GO TO THE
NEXT TENSE

PAST PERFECT
CONTINUOUS TENSE

UNDERSTAND PAST PERFECT CONTINUOUS TENSE

Past Perfect Continuous Tense का उपयोग किसी ऐसे कार्य (action) को व्यक्त करने के लिए किया जाता है जो अतीत में किसी समय से जारी था और किसी अन्य कार्य से पहले तक चलता रहा।

Positive (सकारात्मक):

Subject + had been + Verb (ing) + Object + since/for + time.

Example: She had been studying for two hours.

(वह दो घंटे से पढ़ रही थी।)

Negative (नकारात्मक):

Subject + had not been + Verb (ing) + Object + since/for + time.

Example: She had not been studying for two hours.

(वह दो घंटे से नहीं पढ़ रही थी।)

Interrogative (प्रश्नवाचक):

Had + Subject + been + Verb (ing) + Object + since/for + time?

Example: Had she been studying for two hours?

(क्या वह दो घंटे से पढ़ रही थी?)

PAST PERFECT CONTINUOUS

- वह तीन घंटे से मदद कर रहा था। **(had been helping)**
- वे सुबह से खेत में काम कर रहे थे। **(had been working)**
- शिक्षक दो साल से पढ़ा रहे थे। **(had been teaching)**
- वह एक घंटे से सफाई नहीं कर रहा था। **(had not been cleaning)**
- पौधे कई महीनों से नहीं बढ़ रहे थे। **(had not been growing)**
- लोग वर्षों से खुद को सुधार नहीं रहे थे। **(had not been reforming)**
- वे सुबह से लड़ाई नहीं कर रहे थे। **(had not been fighting)**
- क्या वे शाम से आनंद ले रहे थे? **(Had they been enjoying)**
- क्या वह सुबह से प्रार्थना कर रहा था? **(Had he been praying)**
- क्या शिक्षक छात्रों को दो महीने से दंड दे रहे थे? **(Had the teacher been punishing)**
- क्या वह दोपहर से गाड़ी चला रहा था? **(Had he been driving)**

PAST PERFECT CONTINUOUS

- He **had been helping** for three hours.
- They **had been working** in the field since morning.
- The teacher **had been teaching** for two years.
- He **had not been cleaning** for an hour.
- The plants **had not been growing** for several months.
- People **had not been reforming** themselves for years.
- They **had not been fighting** since morning.
- **Had** they **been enjoying** since evening?
- **Had he been praying** since morning?
- **Had the teacher been punishing** students for two months?
- **Had he been driving** since noon?

Practice Time 1

- वह दो घंटे से इस विषय पर चर्चा कर रहा है। **(discuss)**
- वे सुबह से बैठक की व्यवस्था कर रहे हैं। **(arrange)**
- वह एक घंटे से मुझे मनाने की कोशिश कर रहा है। **(convince)**
- डिलीवरी बॉय आधे घंटे से पार्सल पहुंचा रहा है। **(deliver)**
- वह कई दिनों से मेरी बातों को नजरअंदाज कर रहा है। **(ignore)**
- नृत्य समूह सुबह से मंच पर प्रदर्शन कर रहा है। **(perform)**
- अनुवादक पिछले एक घंटे से इस पुस्तक का अनुवाद कर रहा है। **(translate)**
- छात्र कक्षा में आधे घंटे से शिक्षक की बात बीच में टोक रहे हैं। **(interrupt)**
- वैज्ञानिक कई महीनों से इस समस्या का विश्लेषण कर रहे हैं। **(analyze)**
- वह वर्षों से नई तकनीक का आविष्कार कर रहा है। **(invent)**

English Version 1

- He **has been discussing** this topic for two hours.
- They **have been arranging** the meeting since morning.
- He **has been trying** to convince me for an hour.
- The delivery boy **has been delivering** the parcel for half an hour.
- He **has been ignoring** my words for several days.
- The dance group **has been performing** on stage since morning.
- The translator **has been translating** this book for the past hour.
- The students **have been interrupting** the teacher in class for half an hour.
- Scientists **have been analyzing** this problem for several months.
- He **has been inventing** new technology for years.

Practice Time 2

- वह एक महीने से पैसे उधार नहीं ले रहा था। **(not borrow)**
- वे सुबह से अपनी समस्या की शिकायत नहीं कर रहे थे। **(not complain)**
- वह कई वर्षों से अपने स्वास्थ्य को बनाए नहीं रख रहा था। **(not maintain)**
- वैज्ञानिक कई दिनों से कोई नई खोज नहीं कर रहे थे। **(not discover)**
- लोग उसकी मेहनत की सराहना नहीं कर रहे थे। **(not appreciate)**
- कैदी दो घंटे से भागने की कोशिश नहीं कर रहा था। **(not escape)**
- वह कई दिनों से बीमार होने का ढोंग नहीं कर रहा था। **(not pretend)**
- कंपनी एक साल से उत्पाद की गारंटी नहीं दे रही थी। **(not guarantee)**
- वह कई दिनों से मुझे इस काम के लिए राज़ी नहीं कर रहा था। **(not persuade)**
- डॉक्टर एक घंटे से मशीन को संचालित नहीं कर रहे थे। **(not operate)**

- He **had not been borrowing** money for a month.
- They **had not been complaining** about their problem since morning.
- He **had not been maintaining** his health for many years.
- Scientists **had not been discovering** anything new for several days.
- People **had not been appreciating** his hard work.
- The prisoner **had not been trying** to escape for two hours.
- He **had not been pretending** to be sick for several days.
- The company **had not been guaranteeing** the product for a year.
- He **had not been persuading** me to do this work for several days.
- The doctor **had not been operating** the machine for an hour.

Practice Time 3

- क्या वे एक घंटे से इस विषय पर चर्चा कर रहे थे? **(Discuss)**
- क्या वह सुबह से बैठक की व्यवस्था कर रहा था? **(Arrange)**
- क्या शिक्षक दो दिन से छात्रों को समझाने की कोशिश कर रहे थे? **(Convince)**
- क्या डिलीवरी बॉय आधे घंटे से पार्सल पहुंचा रहा था? **(Deliver)**
- क्या वह कई दिनों से तुम्हारी बातों को नजरअंदाज कर रहा था? **(Ignore)**
- क्या वे सुबह से मंच पर प्रदर्शन कर रहे थे? **(Perform)**
- क्या अनुवादक पिछले एक घंटे से इस पुस्तक का अनुवाद कर रहा था? **(Translate)**
- क्या छात्र कक्षा में आधे घंटे से शिक्षक की बात बीच में टोक रहे थे? **(Interrupt)**
- क्या वैज्ञानिक कई महीनों से इस समस्या का विश्लेषण कर रहे थे? **(Analyze)**
- क्या वह वर्षों से नई तकनीक का आविष्कार कर रहा था? **(Invent)**

English Version 3

- **Had they been discussing** this topic for an hour?
- **Had he been arranging** the meeting since morning?
- **Had the teacher been trying** to convince the students for two days?
- **Had the delivery boy been delivering** the parcel for half an hour?
- **Had he been ignoring** your words for several days?
- **Had they been performing** on stage since morning?
- **Had the translator been translating** this book for the past hour?
- **Had the students been interrupting** the teacher in class for half an hour?
- **Had the scientists been analyzing** this problem for several months?
- **Had he been inventing** new technology for years?

Structure of Past Perfect Continuous Tense

Subject	Had Been	Verb+ing	Object	Since/For	Time Duration
I	had been	reading	the novel	for	two hours
She	had been	practicing	the piano	since	morning
They	had been	playing	football	for	three hours
He	had been	watching	movies	since	evening
We	had been	exploring	the forest	for	several days
The teacher	had been	explaining	the topic	since	first period
Joy	had been	helping	his mother	for	a long time
The children	had been	drawing	pictures	since	10 a.m.
My father	had been	fixing	the car	for	two hours

Structure of Past Perfect Continuous Tense

Subject	Had Not Been	Verb+ing	Object	Since /For	Time Duration
I	had not been	sleeping	well	for	a few days
She	had not been	attending	classes	since	Monday
They	had not been	talking	to each other	for	a week
Joy	had not been	taking	his medicines	since	morning
The child	had not been	eating	properly	for	three days
Subject	Had Not Been	Verb+ing	Object	Since/For	Time Duration
I	had not been	sleeping	well	for	a few days
She	had not been	attending	classes	since	Monday
They	had not been	talking	to each other	for	a week

तीन दिनों से बारिश हो रही थी। सड़कों पर पिछली रात से पानी भर रहा था। लोग कई घंटों से भीगने से बचने के लिए घरों में रह रहे थे।

तीन दिनों से बारिश हो रही थी। सड़कों पर पिछली रात से पानी भर रहा था। लोग कई घंटों से भीगने से बचने के लिए घरों में रह रहे थे।

raining, flooding, staying, waiting, shaking, worrying

Speak English - 13

It had been raining for three days. The streets had been flooding since the previous night. People had been staying indoors for hours to avoid getting wet. The children had been waiting eagerly for the rain to stop since morning. The strong winds had been shaking the trees for several hours. The farmers had been worrying about their crops for the past two days.

What problems had people been facing for two days due to heavy rain?

जॉय दस मिनट से अपने सहपाठियों से अनुशासन में बैठने का अनुरोध कर रहा था। वह पिछले पाँच मिनट से शांत बनाए रखने के महत्व को समझा रहा था। कुछ छात्र कई मिनटों से उसके बार-बार अनुरोध करने के बावजूद आपस में फुसफुसा रहे थे। शिक्षक पिछले कुछ क्षणों से दरवाजे से उनके व्यवहार को देख रहे थे। कुछ ज़िम्मेदार छात्र पिछले दस मिनट से जॉय के प्रयासों का समर्थन कर रहे थे। हालांकि, शरारती छात्र शिक्षक के जाने के बाद से ही कक्षा में गड़बड़ी पैदा कर रहे थे।

Joy had been requesting his classmates to sit in discipline for ten minutes. He had been explaining the importance of maintaining silence for the past five minutes. Some students had been whispering to each other despite his repeated requests for several minutes. The teacher had been observing their behavior from the doorway for the last few moments. A few responsible students had been supporting Joy's efforts to maintain discipline for the past ten minutes. However, the mischievous ones had been creating disturbances in the classroom since the teacher left.

Did you ever mind your class?

जॉय और उसकी टीम एक हफ्ते से अंतिम सामान्य ज्ञान परीक्षा की तैयारी कर रही थी। वे पिछले पाँच दिनों से इतिहास और विज्ञान के विषय पढ़ रहे थे। उनके शिक्षक सोमवार से उन्हें मॉक टेस्ट करवा रहे थे। टीम हर शाम कई घंटे से जरूरी बातें दोहरा रही थी। कुछ सदस्य पिछले कुछ दिनों से करेंट अफेयर्स समझने में दिक्कत महसूस कर रहे थे। फिर भी, वे पिछले एक हफ्ते से अपनी तैयारी में सुधार कर रहे थे।

practice, study, guide, revise, struggle, improve,

Speak English - 15

Joy and his team had been practicing for the final general knowledge test for a week. They had been studying various topics from history and science for the past five days. Their mentor had been guiding them through mock tests since Monday. The team had been revising important facts and figures for several hours each evening. Some members had been struggling with current affairs for the last few days. Despite the challenges, they had been improving their accuracy and speed over the past week.

What do you do to improve your general knowledge?

जॉय सुबह से अपनी माँ का स्केच बना रहा था। यह उसकी माँ का जन्मदिन था, और वह उन्हें कुछ खास उपहार देना चाहता था। वह पिछले कुछ दिनों से

विभिन्न shading तकनीकों का अभ्यास कर रहा था। वह कई घंटों से पुरानी पारिवारिक तस्वीरों से प्रेरणा ले रहा था। वह दोपहर से उनकी आँखों के बारीक विवरण पर ध्यानपूर्वक काम कर रहा था। वह पिछली रात से ही उनकी प्रतिक्रिया की कल्पना कर रहा था।

वह रात से ही सोच रहा था कि माँ इसे देखकर कैसी प्रतिक्रिया देंगी।

draw, was, wanted, practice, gathering, working, imagining

Speak English - 16

Joy had been drawing a sketch of his mother since morning. It was his mother's birthday, and he wanted to

gift her something special. He had been practicing different shading techniques for the past few days. He had been gathering inspiration from old family photos for several hours. He had been carefully working on the fine details of her eyes since noon. He had been imagining her reaction to the gift since the previous night.

What you did to make your mother feel happy on her birthday?

जॉय पिछले हफ्ते से अपनी बहन के लिए एक गाना तैयार कर रहा था। यह उसकी ग्रेजुएशन का दिन था और वह उसे एक दिल छू लेने वाली धुन से सरप्राइज देना चाहता था। वह कई दिनों से अलग-अलग धुनों पर प्रयोग कर रहा था। वह सोमवार से ऐसे सुंदर बोल लिख रहा था, जो उनके बचपन की यादों को दर्शाते थे। वह घंटों से अपने गिटार पर कॉर्ड्स का अभ्यास कर रहा था। वह यह सब अपनी बहन से छुपाकर कर रहा था।

compose, want, experiment, write, practice, do, keep

Speak English - 17

Joy had been composing a song for his sister since last week. It was her graduation day and he wanted to surprise her with a heartfelt melody. He had been experimenting with different tunes for several days. He had been writing meaningful lyrics that captured their childhood memories since Monday. He had been practicing the chords on his guitar for hours. He had been doing it while keeping it a secret from his sister.

Tell your fond memory with your brother or sister

दो हफ्तों से बसंत का मौसम था। पूरे वातावरण ने एक नया रूप ले लिया था। फूल खूबसूरती से खिल रहे थे, चारों ओर रंग भर रहे थे। पक्षी खुशी से चहचहा रहे थे, जैसे कोई मीठा गीत गा रहे हों। हल्की हवा पत्तों से धीरे-धीरे बातें कर रही थी, जिससे वे नाचने लगे। सुनहरी धूप नरमी से चमक रही थी, जिससे सब कुछ उजला और सुंदर लग रहा था। सच में, बसंत ने दुनिया को ताजगी और खूबसूरती से भर दिया था।

had been, got, blooming, filling, chirping, singing, whispering, shining, making, made

Speak English - 18

It had been spring for two weeks. The whole environment had got a new face. Flowers had been blooming beautifully, filling the surroundings with colors. The birds had been chirping happily, as if singing a sweet song. The gentle breeze had been whispering secrets to the dancing leaves. The golden sun had been shining warmly, making everything look bright and lovely. Truly, spring had made the world fresh and beautiful.

Had the arrival of spring been making the surroundings more lively and colorful for the past two weeks?

समाज के लिए यह एक चुनौतीपूर्ण समय था। बेरोजगारी कई महीनों से बढ़ रही थी, जिससे कई लोग अपनी जरूरतें पूरी करने के लिए संघर्ष कर रहे थे। अपराध दर बढ़ रही थी, जिससे लोग अपने ही मोहल्लों में असुरक्षित महसूस कर रहे थे। प्रदूषण हवा और पानी को प्रभावित कर रहा था, जिससे गंभीर स्वास्थ्य समस्याएँ हो रही थीं। शिक्षा की खाई बढ़ रही थी, जिससे गरीबों के लिए अच्छा भविष्य बनाना और मुश्किल हो रहा था। सच में, समाज कई समस्याओं का सामना कर रहा था, जिन्हें तुरंत हल करने की जरूरत थी।

challenging, rising, leaving, increasing, feel, affecting, causing, widening, making, facing

Speak English - 19

It had been a challenging time for society. Unemployment had been rising for several months, leaving many struggling to meet their needs. Crime rates had been increasing, making people feel unsafe in their own neighborhoods. Pollution had been affecting the air and water, causing serious health issues. Education gaps had been widening, making it harder for the poor to build a better future. Truly, society had been facing many problems that needed urgent solutions.

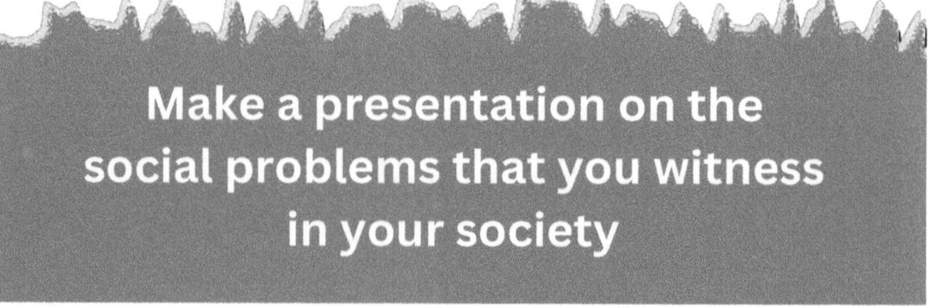

हफ्तों से शादी का मौसम था। पूरे माहौल में खुशी और उत्सव की चमक थी। परिवार अपने घरों को रंग-बिरंगी रोशनी और फूलों से सजा रहे थे। पारंपरिक

संगीत की धुनें हवा में गूंज रही थीं, जिससे हर कोई खुशी से नाच रहा था। दूल्हा-दुल्हन शुभ रस्में निभा रहे थे, अपने नए सफर के लिए आशीर्वाद ले रहे थे। स्वादिष्ट भोजन की खुशबू हर तरफ फैल रही थी, जिससे हर मेहमान ललचा रहा था। सच में, शादियां सबके लिए खुशी और अपनापन ला रही थीं।

got, decorating, filling, making, following, seeking, spreading, tempting, bringing

Speak English - 20

It had been a wedding season for weeks. The whole atmosphere had got a festive touch. Families had been decorating their homes with colorful lights and flowers. The sound of traditional music had been filling the air, making everyone dance with joy. The bride and groom had been following the sacred rituals, seeking blessings for their new journey. The aroma of delicious food had been

spreading every where, tempting every guest. Truly, weddings had been bringing happiness and togetherness to all.

एक समय था जब लोग ऐसे समाज में रहते थे जहाँ चोरी या अपराध का कोई भय नहीं था। ईमानदार शासकों ने ऐसा तंत्र स्थापित किया था जहाँ न्याय सही तरीके से किया जाता था। लोग शांति से रह थे और बिना किसी संदेह के एक-दूसरे

पर भरोसा करते थे। व्यापारी अपनी दुकानें खुली छोड़ देते थे और यात्री निश्चिंत

होकर घूमते थे। लेकिन समय के साथ, लालच और बेईमानी एक भेड़ की खाल में भेड़िया बनकर समाज में घुस गई और वह सुनहरा युग समाप्त हो गया।

lived, was, established, served,
living, trusting, leaving, roaming,
passed, crept, faded away

There was a time when people lived in a society where there was no fear of theft or crime. The honest rulers had established a system where justice had been served fairly. People had been living peacefully, trusting each other without doubt. Merchants had been leaving their shops open and travelers had been roaming freely without worry. But as time passed, greed and dishonesty had crept in like a wolf in sheep's clothing and that golden era faded away.

एक हीरा व्यापारी एक महीने से यात्रा कर रहा था और उसके पास कई कीमती रत्न और जवाहरात थे। एक रात तेज़ बारिश हो रही थी, इसलिए उसे एक सराय में शरण लेनी पड़ी। एक चोर, जो उसे पीछा कर रहा था, उसी कमरे में ठहरा क्योंकि कोई और कमरा उपलब्ध नहीं था। चोर अवसर की तलाश में था और अंततः रात में व्यापारी के बैग तलाशे, लेकिन कुछ नहीं मिला। अगले दिन सुबह, उसने अपनी मंशा कबूल की और कीमती चीजों के बारे में पूछा। व्यापारी मुस्कुराया और बताया कि उसने उन्हें चोर के ही बैग में रखा था!

travelling, carrying, raining, following, stayed, waiting, searched, found, admitted, smiled, revealed, kept

Speak English - 22

A diamond merchant had been traveling for a month, carrying precious stones and gems. One night, it had been raining heavily, so he had to take shelter in an inn. A thief, who had been following him, stayed in the same room as no other was available. The thief had been waiting for a chance and finally searched the merchant's bags at night but found nothing. The next morning, he admitted his intentions and asked

where the valuables were. The merchant smiled and revealed he had kept them in the thief's own bag!

एक बुद्धिमान राजा कई वर्षों से अपने राज्य पर शांति से शासन कर रहा था। एक दिन, दो लोगों के बीच एक घोड़े को लेकर विवाद हो रहा था, दोनों उस पर

अपना अधिकार जता रहे थे। राजा धैर्यपूर्वक सुन रहा था और फिर उसने एक परीक्षा का आदेश दिया। उसने दोनों से घोड़े को बुलाने के लिए कहा। घोड़ा स्थिर खड़ा था, लेकिन उत्सुकता से एक आदमी के पास दौड़ गया। राजा मुस्कुराया और उसे सच्चा मालिक घोषित किया, क्योंकि असली बंधन को झुठलाया नहीं जा सकता था। इस प्रकार, न्याय बुद्धिमानी से किया गया।

ruling, going on, listening, asked, standing, ran, smiled, declared, served

Speak English - 23

A wise king had been ruling his kingdom peacefully for many years. One day, a dispute had been going on between two men over a horse, each claiming ownership. The king had been listening patiently and then ordered a test. He asked both men to call the horse. The horse had been standing still but ran to one man eagerly. The king smiled and declared him the true owner, as only a real bond could not be faked. Justice had been served wisely, proving the king's wisdom once again.

एक बुद्धिमान वृद्ध व्यक्ति कई वर्षों से एक छोटे से गाँव में रह रहे थे और अपनी बुद्धि से लोगों का मार्गदर्शन कर रहे थे। एक शाम, एक युवा व्यक्ति, जो असफलताओं से जूझ रहा था, उनसे सलाह लेने आया। सुबह से ही बारिश हो रही थी और वे एक आश्रय के नीचे बैठ गए। युवा व्यक्ति अपनी बदकिस्मती की शिकायत करने लगा। वृद्ध व्यक्ति मुस्कुराए और उसे एक बीज दिया, कहते हुए, "इसे बोओ और रोज़ पानी दो।"

युवा व्यक्ति महीनों तक उसे सींचता रहा, लेकिन कुछ भी नहीं उगा। वह हताश महसूस करने लगा, लेकिन जैसे ही वह हार मानने ही वाला था, उसने देखा कि पौधे में फूल खिलने लगे। यह धैर्य का सबक था— सफलता पहले अदृश्य रूप से बढ़ती है, फिर खिलती है!

living, guiding, struggling, came, raining, sat, complained, smiled, nurturing, grew, felt, noticed, grows

Speak English - 24

A wise old man had been living in a small village for years, guiding people with his wisdom. One

evening, a young man, who had been struggling with failures, came to him for advice. It had been raining since morning, and they sat under a shelter. The young man complained about his bad luck. The old man smiled and gave him a seed, saying, "Plant this and water it daily." The young man had been nurturing it for months, but nothing grew. He felt frustrated, but no sooner was he about to give up than he noticed blossoms. This was a lesson in patience—success grows unseen before it blooms!

एक समय था जब महान आर्थिक मंदी महीनों से लाखों लोगों को प्रभावित कर रही थी। व्यवसाय बंद हो रहे थे, और बेरोजगारी तेजी से बढ़ रही थी। एक युवा व्यक्ति, जो काम की तलाश में संघर्ष कर रहा था, रोज़ मीलों पैदल चलता था। एक शाम, वह एक फैक्ट्री के बाहर इंतजार कर रहा था, जब उसने एक गुप्त vacancy के

बारे में सुना। बिना देर किए, वह प्रबंधक के कार्यालय पहुंचा और नौकरी पा ली। बाद में, वह

मुस्कुराया, यह महसूस करते हुए कि धैर्य ही उन कठिन समय में उसकी सबसे बड़ी ताकत थी!

affecting, collapsing, rising, struggling, walked, waiting, overheard, reached, got hired, smiled

Speak English - 25

There was a time when the Great Depression had been affecting millions for months. 

Businesses had been collapsing, and unemployment had been rising rapidly. A young man, who had been struggling to find work, walked miles daily in search of a job. One evening, he had been waiting outside a factory when he overheard about a secret vacancy. Without delay, he reached the manager's office and got hired. Later, he smiled, realizing that patience had been his greatest strength during those tough times!

अवनी चतुर्वेदी सालों से भारतीय वायु सेना में लिंग की बाधाओं को तोड़ रही थीं, इससे पहले कि वह अकेले लड़ाकू विमान उड़ाने वाली पहली महिला पायलटों में से एक बनीं। मध्य प्रदेश में जन्मी, उन्हें बचपन से ही उड़ान का शौक था और उन्होंने अपने सपने को पूरा करने के लिए कड़ी मेहनत की। उन्होंने कई युवा महिलाओं को आत्मविश्वास के साथ रक्षा बलों में शामिल होने के लिए प्रेरित किया। जैसा कि वह साबित करती हैं, "आसमान सीमा नहीं है, यह तो बस शुरुआत है।"

breaking, became, had been, worked, inspiring, proves

Avani Chaturvedi had been breaking gender barriers in the Indian Air Force for years before she became one of the first female fighter pilots to fly a combat aircraft alone. Born in Madhya Pradesh, she had been passionate about flying since childhood and worked hard to achieve her dream. She had been inspiring many young women to join the defense forces with confidence. As she proves, "The sky is not the limit; it's just the beginning."

हेलेन केलर बचपन से ही अंधेरे और सन्नाटे में जी रही थीं, क्योंकि एक बीमारी ने उनकी आँखों की रोशनी और सुनने की शक्ति छीन ली थी। फिर भी, उन्होंने हार नहीं मानी। उनकी शिक्षिका ऐनी सुलिवन ने उन्हें स्पर्श और इशारों की भाषा के जरिए संवाद करना सिखाया। उन्होंने साबित किया कि सच्ची ताकत मन में होती है। बाद में, वह लेखिका, समाजसेवी और वक्ता बनीं, जिन्होंने लाखों लोगों को प्रेरित किया। "अंधेपन से भी बुरा है, नजरें तो हों लेकिन कोई लक्ष्य न हो।"

living, took away, determined, learned, proving, became,

Helen Keller had been living in darkness and silence since childhood, as an illness took away her sight

and hearing. Yet, she had been determined to overcome her challenges. With the guidance of her teacher, Anne Sullivan, she learned to communicate using touch and sign language. She had been proving that disability cannot stop a determined mind. Later, she became a writer, activist, and speaker, inspiring millions worldwide. "The only thing worse than being blind is having sight but no vision."

वो दिन बहुत सुन्दर था । मैं चाहता हूँ की वैसा दिन जीवन में बार बार आये। जीवन के ग्यारह बरस मैं बिता चुका था। ये मेरा बारहवा जनम दिन था।मेरी ख्वाहिश थी की दूसरे दोस्तो की तरह मेरे पास भी एक साईकिल हो। परन्तु पिता जी की आर्थिक स्थिति के कारण मैंने कभी अपनी इच्छा जाहिर नही की। जैसे कहा जाता है 'जहा चाह वहा राह'। हमारे स्कूल ने सामान्य ज्ञान की परीक्षा का आयोजन किया। जितने वाले के लिए इनाम था चमचमाता लाल साईकिल। पिता जी अपनी आमदनी से साईकिल ले कर नहीं दे सकते थे पर मैं तो अपने ज्ञान को बड़ा कर उसे पाने की कोशिश तो कर ही सकता था। मैंने कुछ सामान्य ज्ञान की पुस्तके पढ़ना शुरू किया और रोज अखबार पढ़ना मेरी दिनचर्या बन गयी। मेरे मेहनत रंग लाई। एक के बाद एक सभी पड़ाव को मैंने पार किया और चमचमाती लाल साईकिल का अधिकारी बना।

was, would come, spent, wished, expressed, organized, afford, try, started reading, paid off

Speak English - 28

That day was very beautiful. I wish such a day would come again and again in my life. I had already spent eleven years of my life, and this was my twelfth birthday. I wished to have a bicycle like my other friends, but due to my father's financial condition, I never expressed my desire. As it is said, "Where there is a will, there is a way." Our school organized a general knowledge competition, and the prize for the winner was a sparkling red bicycle. My father could not afford to buy me a bicycle, but I could at least try to win it by increasing my knowledge.

I started reading general knowledge books and made it a habit to read the newspaper daily. My hard work paid off. I cleared one stage after another and finally became the proud winner of the sparkling red bicycle.

समाज में अतीत में कई बुरी प्रथाएँ प्रचलित थीं। उनमें से एक थी बाल विवाह। गीता, एक चमकती आँखों वाली पाँच साल की बच्ची, अपनी गुड़ियों से खेलने में मग्न रहती थी। लेकिन एक दिन उसकी दुनिया बदल गई—उसे दुल्हन की तरह सजाया गया और उसका विवाह कर दिया गया। घबराई और डरी हुई गीता अपनी माँ से लिपट गई, यह समझने में असमर्थ कि क्या हो रहा था। उसके स्कूल जाने के सपने खो गए और उनकी जगह खामोशी और कर्तव्यों ने ले ली। सालों बाद, सामाजिक सुधारों ने कई बच्चियों को इस प्रथा से मुक्त कर दिया, लेकिन गीता का छीना हुआ बचपन उसके दिल में एक अनकही पीड़ा बनकर रह गया।

prevailing, loved, changed, married off, clung, happening, faded, replaced, freed, remained

Many evil practices had been prevailing in the society for a long time in our society in the past. One of them was child marriage. Gitu, a bright-eyed five-year-old, loved playing with her dolls. But one day, her world changed—she was dressed as a bride and married off. Confused and scared, she clung to her mother, unaware of what was happening. Her dreams of school faded, replaced by silence and duties. Years later, social reforms freed many like her, but Gitu's stolen childhood remained an unspoken wound in her heart.

रीना बचपन से ही एक डांसर बनने का सपना देख रही थी। वह हर शाम अपने छोटे से कमरे में अभ्यास कर रही थी, बड़े मंच की

कल्पना करते हुए। वह सालों से कड़ी मेहनत कर रही थी, लेकिन दुर्भाग्यवश, एक दुर्घटना में उसने अपना एक पैर खो दिया। टूटने के बावजूद, वह अपने संकल्प से अपनी ताकत फिर से बना रही थी। उसका जुनून न केवल उसे नाम और शोहरत तक ले गया, बल्कि उसने अपनी डांस अकादमी में कई लोगों को प्रशिक्षित भी किया। **"जीवन की कठिनाइयाँ हमें नष्ट करने नहीं, बल्कि हमारे भीतर छुपी क्षमता को उजागर करने के लिए आती हैं।"**

dreaming, practicing, imagining, working, lost, rebuilding, led, helped, do not come to destroy, help us realize

Speak English - 30

Reena had been dreaming of becoming a dancer since childhood. She had been practicing every evening in her small room, imagining a big stage. She had been working hard for years, but unfortunately, she lost one leg in an accident. Though shattered, she had been rebuilding her strength with determination. Her passion not only led her to name and fame but also helped her train many in her dance academy. **"Difficulties in life do not come to destroy us but to help us realize your hidden potential."**

Fill-in-the-blank sentences using past tenses.

1. She _____ (**undertake**) a challenging project despite the risks.
2. They _____ (**strive**) for excellence in every task.
3. The scientist _____ (**forecast**) the possible outcomes of the experiment for a month.
4. He _____ (**withhold**) crucial information during the meeting.
5. The team _____ (**collaborate**) effectively to meet the deadline.
6. When I arrived, they _____ (**negotiate**) the terms of the contract.
7. She _____ (**contemplate**) a career change for months.
8. By the time we reached, the guests _____ (**depart**) already.
9. The manager _____ (**delegate**) responsibilities wisely.
10. They _____ (**disrupt**) the entire workflow with their sudden decision.
11. He _____ (**articulate**) his vision clearly in the presentation.
12. The employees _____ (**adhere**) to the company policies strictly since Morning.

1. She **undertook** a challenging project despite the risks.
2. They **strove** for excellence in every task.
3. The scientist **had been forecasting** the possible outcomes of the experiment for a month.
4. He **withheld** crucial information during the meeting.
5. The team **collaborated** effectively to meet the deadline.
6. When I **arrived**, they **were negotiating** the terms of the contract.
7. She **had been contemplating** a career change for months.
8. By the time we **reached,** the guests **had departed** already.
9. The manager **delegated** responsibilities wisely.
10. They **disrupted** the entire workflow with their sudden decision.
11. He **articulated** his vision clearly in the presentation.
12. The employees **had been adhering** to the company policies strictly since Morning.

1. बिल्ली कोने में सो रही थी और चूहे दो घंटे से कमरे में इधर-उधर दौड़ रहे थे।

2. बारिश हो रही थी और बच्चे सुबह से कीचड़ में खेल रहे थे।

3. मैं किताब पढ़ रहा था जबकि मेरी बहन दो घंटे से खाना पका रही थी।

4. पिता जी अखबार पढ़ रहे थे और मां सुबह से रसोई में व्यस्त थीं।

5. वह रास्ते में चल रहा था जबकि उसके दोस्त काफी देर से उसका इंतज़ार कर रहे थे।

6. ट्रेन प्लेटफॉर्म पर खड़ी थी और यात्री कई घंटों से अपनी सीटों का इंतजार कर रहे थे।

7. मैं मोबाइल चला रहा था और नेटवर्क दोपहर से खराब चल रहा था।

8. टीचर पढ़ा रहे थे और कुछ छात्र सुबह से क्लास के बाहर खड़े थे।

9. सूरज डूब रहा था और पक्षी बहुत देर से अपने घोंसले में लौट रहे थे।

10. हम मंदिर जा रहे थे जबकि पुजारी जी कई घंटे से पूजा कर रहे थे।

11. वह फिल्म देख रही थी और उसका भाई दोपहर से गेम खेल रहा था।

12. दादी कहानी सुना रही थीं और बच्चे काफी देर से ध्यान से सुन रहे थे।

Practice Time

1. दो साल से बारिश नहीं हुई थी, किसान तब से बारिश के लिए प्रार्थना कर रहे थे।
2. हम स्कूल पहुँच चुके थे, लेकिन शिक्षक तब से क्लास में पढ़ा रहे थे।
3. दादी सो चुकी थीं, लेकिन बच्चे देर से तक कहानियाँ सुनने की जिद कर रहे थे।
4. ट्रेन छूट चुकी थी, और यात्री घंटों से टिकट खिड़की पर खड़े थे।
5. डॉक्टर आ चुके थे, लेकिन मरीज सुबह से दर्द की शिकायत कर रहा था।
6. हम खाना खा चुके थे, लेकिन माँ तब से मिठाई बना रही थीं।
7. पंखा बंद हो चुका था, और बिजली कई घंटों से जा रही थी।
8. बारिश रुक चुकी थी, लेकिन लोग तब से छतरी लेकर घूम रहे थे।
9. गाड़ी रवाना हो चुकी थी, और चालक काफी देर से हॉर्न बजा रहा था।
10. परीक्षा समाप्त हो चुकी थी, लेकिन छात्र तब से उत्तर पत्रिका को देख रहे थे।
11. पुलिस आ चुकी थी, लेकिन पड़ोसी तब से शोर के बारे में शिकायत कर रहे थे।
12. फिल्म शुरू हो चुकी थी, लेकिन दर्शक तब से अपनी सीटें ढूंढ रहे थे।

1. Had he been delivering the speech for an hour before the mic stopped working?
2. Had they been following the new strategy before the policy changed?
3. Had the team been discussing the merger for weeks before announcing it?
4. Had she been contemplating a career switch before she resigned?
5. Had the mentor been guiding the students for months before the final exam?
6. Had the mountaineers been climbing the peak for days before the storm hit?
7. Had the students been comprehending the concept before the teacher moved to the next topic?
8. Had the leader been galvanizing his team before the project deadline?
9. Had they been facilitating the workshop effectively before the technical issues occurred?
10. Had she been perceiving the situation differently before hearing both sides?

1. Had you **already jumped the gun** (acted too soon) before hearing the full instructions?
2. Had they **burnt the midnight oil** (worked late into the night) to finish the project before the deadline?
3. Had you **let the cat out of the bag** (revealed a secret) before the surprise party began?
4. Had your friends **missed the boat** (lost an opportunity) by ignoring the early registration offer?
5. Had you **taken the bull by the horns** (dealt with a problem directly) before the situation worsened?
6. Had he kept his nose to the grindstone (worked hard and continuously) to achieve the promotion?
7. Had she **thrown in the towel** (given up) before even attempting the last round?
8. Had we already put all our eggs in one basket (relied on a single plan) before considering other options?
9. Had you **turned a blind eye** (ignored something intentionally) to the warnings before facing the consequences?
10. Had they been on cloud nine (felt extremely happy) after receiving the good news?

Describe The Oops Jobs Joy Had Been Doing for a week.

For example :

- **Joy had been forgetting homework notebook at home**
- **He had been using his pet's plate for his meal.**
- **He had been watering artificial plants.**

COOKING PASTA

- How long had the snake charmer been showing the snake dance?
- What had the man with puppets been doing before people came?
- How long had the dancers been dancing on the stage?

- Melting the Chocolate
- Preparing the Ice Cream Bars
- Dipping in Chocolate Coating
- Packing the Choco Bars

PRACTICE WORKSHEET

- She __________ (cook) dinner for an hour before the guests arrived.
- They __________ (play) cricket all afternoon when it started to rain.
- I __________ (wait) for you since 10 o'clock!
- He __________ (work) on that machine before it broke down.
- The children __________ (watch) cartoons until their mom turned off the TV.
- We __________ (clean) the house before the guests came.
- You __________ (study) English for a year before you gave the test.
- My friends __________ (travel) for days before they reached the city.
- The painter __________ (paint) the wall when we arrived.
- It __________ (rain) for hours before the sun came out.
- The dog __________ (bark) loudly before its owner took it inside.
- I __________ (read) a mystery novel before I lost interest.

WORKSHEET ANSWER

- She **had been cooking** dinner for an hour before the guests arrived.
- They **had been playing** cricket all afternoon when it started to rain.
- I **had been waiting** for you since 10 o'clock!
- He **had been working** on that machine before it broke down.
- The children **had been watching** cartoons until their mom turned off the TV.
- We **had been cleaning** the house before the guests came.
- You **had been studying** English for a year before you gave the test.
- My friends **had been traveling** for days before they reached the city.
- The painter **had been painting** the wall when we arrived.
- It **had been raining** for hours before the sun came out.
- The **dog had been barking** loudly before its owner took it inside.
- I **had been reading** a mystery novel before I lost interest.

CORRECT THE MISTAKES

- She is go to school when it started to rain.
- I have saw that movie already.
- They was playing football since morning.
- He don't know the answer to that question.
- By next year, she has completed her degree.
- The boys plays outside every evening.
- I am living here since 2015.
- She will buys a new car next month.
- We had went to the museum before it closed.
- He working on his project right now.
- When I arrived, they eat their lunch.
- The teacher is explaining the lesson before the bell rang.

- She **was going** to school when it started to rain.
- I **have seen** that movie already.
- They **had been playing** football since morning.
- He **doesn't know** the answer to that question.
- By next year, she **will have completed** her degree.
- The boys **play** outside every evening.
- I **have been living** here since 2015.
- She **will buy** a new car next month.
- We **had gone** to the museum before it closed.
- He **is working** on his project right now.
- When I arrived, they **were eating** their lunch.
- The teacher **had been explaining** the lesson before the bell rang.

COMPLETE THE SENTENCES MEANINGFULLY

- The children had been waiting for the bus at the bus stop for half an hour because _____________________.
- She had been studying in the library for three hours although _____________________.
- We had been cleaning the house since morning as _____________________.
- I had been practicing the piano daily even though _____________________.
- The workers had been repairing the road all night until _____________________.
- He had been feeling unwell for a week before _____________________.
- They had been traveling through the forest since dawn when suddenly _____________________.
- My parents had been planning a surprise party for days but _____________________.
- The students had been preparing for the play with great enthusiasm while _____________________.
- You had been calling me continuously since last night so _____________________.

- The dog had been barking loudly for an hour because ___________________________.
- Riya had been painting the wall carefully although ___________________________.
- They had been playing football in the rain until ___________________________.
- The teacher had been explaining the topic for a long time but ___________________________.
- I had been reading that novel every night before ___________________________.
- The farmer had been working in the field since early morning when ___________________________.
- We had been waiting at the restaurant for so long as ___________________________.
- He had been jogging every morning even though ___________________________.
- The baby had been crying non-stop for ten minutes because ___________________________.
- The team had been practicing hard for the match although ___________________________.

Make Your Notes

Make Your Notes

Make Your Notes

Make Your Notes

LET'S GO TO THE NEXT TENSE

FUTURE PERFECT CONTINUOUS

UNDERSTAND FUTURE PERFECT CONTINUOUS

Future Perfect Continuous Tense
Subject + will have been + Verb (ing) + Object + समय

नियम (Rules):

1. क्रिया का कोई कार्य भविष्य में किसी निश्चित समय तक जारी रहेगा।

- वह शाम 5 बजे तक तीन घंटे से पढ़ रही होगी।

2. वाक्य में समय का उल्लेख अनिवार्य होता है, जैसे – for two hours, since morning, by next year।

- वे अगले जून तक यहाँ पाँच साल से काम कर रहे होंगे।

3. 'Since' और 'For' का सही उपयोग करना आवश्यक है।

Since – किसी निश्चित समय (Point of Time) के लिए: Since Monday, Since 2010, Since Morning

For – किसी अवधि (Period of Time) के लिए: For two hours, For five years, For a long time

मैं सुबह से तुम्हारा इंतज़ार कर रहा होऊँगा।

UNDERSTAND FUTURE PERFECT CONTINUOUS

Future Perfect Continuous Tense

Subject + will have been + Verb (ing) + Object + समय

4. Interrogative Sentences (प्रश्नवाचक वाक्य):
- Will + Subject + have been + Verb (ing) + Object + समय?
- Example: क्या वह अगले जनवरी तक दस साल से यहाँ रह रही होगी?

5. Negative Sentences (नकारात्मक वाक्य):
Subject + will not have been + Verb (ing) + Object + समय

Example: वह इस प्रोजेक्ट पर दो महीने से काम नहीं कर रहा होगा।
वर्षा ऋतु के आरम्भ से रेगिस्तान में वर्षा नहीं हो रही होगी।

Practice Time 1

- मौसम पिछले कुछ महीनों से अप्रत्याशित रूप से बदलता रहा होगा। **(change)**

- यह किताब एक नए संस्करण के आने तक पीढ़ियों से पाठकों को प्रेरित कर रही होगी। **(inspire)**

- माता-पिता सालों से अपने बच्चों का मार्गदर्शन कर रहे होंगे, इससे पहले कि वे स्वतंत्र हो जाएं। **(guide)**

- वैज्ञानिक 2030 तक दशकों से इस बीमारी का इलाज खोज रहे होंगे। **(research)**

- सबूत अंतिम निर्णय की घोषणा से पहले कई वर्षों से इस सिद्धांत का समर्थन कर रहे होंगे। **(support)**

- अभ्यास प्रतियोगिता तक महीनों से तुम्हारी क्षमताओं को निखार रहा होगा। **(improve)**

- समय हमें पूरी तरह आगे बढ़ने से पहले कई वर्षों से पुराने घावों को भर रहा होगा। **(heal)**

- हमारी परंपराएं अगली पीढ़ी तक सदियों से हमारी संस्कृति को आकार दे रही होंगी। **(shape)**

- तुम्हारी मुस्कान मेरे दिनों को लंबे समय से रोशन कर रही होगी, इससे पहले कि मैं उसके प्रभाव को समझूं। **(brighten)**

- मेरा दिल हमारे फिर से मिलने तक वर्षों से तुम्हारी मौजूदगी के लिए तड़प रहा होगा। **(long)**

- The weather **will have been changing** unpredictably for the past few months.
- The book **will have been inspiring** readers for generations by the time a new edition is released.
- Parents **will have been guiding** their children for years before they become independent.
- Scientists **will have been researching** a cure for this disease for decades by 2030.
- The evidences **will have been supporting** the theory for several years before the final verdict is announced.
- The practice **will have been improving** your skills for months by the time you compete.
- Time **will have been healing** old wounds for years before we truly move on.
- Our traditions **will have been shaping** our culture for centuries by the next generation.
- Your smile **will have been brightening** my days for a long time before I realize its impact.
- My heart **will have been longing** for your presence for years by the time we meet again.

- तूफ़ान तीन घंटे तक नहीं चल रहा होगा जब तक हम घर नहीं पहुँचते। **(rage)**
- यह किताब लंबे समय तक पाठकों को प्रभावित नहीं कर रही होगी जब तक इसे नए संस्करण से नहीं बदला जाता। **(influence)**
- साबूत सालों तक कुछ भी साबित नहीं कर रहे होंगे इससे पहले कि मामला खारिज कर दिया जाए। **(prove)**
- अभ्यास महीनों तक उसकी कौशल में सुधार नहीं कर रहा होगा यदि वह असंगत बना रहता है। **(improve)**
- समय दशकों तक सभी घाव नहीं भर रहा होगा यदि लोग मन में द्वेष बनाए रखते हैं। **(heal)**
- हमारी परंपराएँ सदियों तक लुप्त नहीं हो रही होंगी यदि हम उन्हें संरक्षित करते रहें। **(fade away)**
- तुम्हारा समर्थन सालों तक उनकी मदद नहीं कर रहा होगा यदि तुम इसे वापस लेने का निर्णय लेते हो। **(help)**
- मेरा दिल बहुत लंबे समय तक तुम्हारी लालसा नहीं कर रहा होगा यदि मैं अपने भीतर शांति पा लूँ। **(long for)**

- The storm **will not have been raging** for three hours by the time we reach home.
- The book **will not have been influencing** readers for a long time before it is replaced by a new edition.
- The evidences **will not have been proving** anything for years before the case is dismissed.
- The practice **will not have been improving** his skills for months if he remains inconsistent.
- Time **will not have been healing** all wounds for decades if people keep holding grudges.
- Our traditions **will not have been fading away** for centuries if we continue to preserve them.
- Your support **will not have been helping** them for years if you decide to withdraw it.
- My heart **will not have been longing** for you for too long if I find peace within myself.

- क्या तुम कई घंटों से पढ़ाई कर रहे होगे जब मैं पहुँचूँगा? **(studying)**
- क्या बच्चे शाम तक दो घंटे से पार्क में खेल रहे होंगे? **(playing)**
- क्या उपदेश दशकों से लोगों के विचारों को प्रभावित कर रहे होंगे? **(influencing)**
- क्या बादल सुबह से आकाश को ढक रहे होंगे? **(covering)**
- क्या प्रदूषण वर्षों से लोगों के स्वास्थ्य को प्रभावित कर रहा होगा? **(affecting)**
- क्या सर्दी पिछले कुछ हफ्तों से बर्फबारी ला रही होगी? **(bringing)**
- क्या मेहमान हमारे पहुँचने तक एक घंटे से खाने का इंतजार कर रहे होंगे? **(waiting)**
- क्या पुराने भवन देखभाल की कमी के कारण दशकों से जर्जर हो रहे होंगे? **(deteriorating)**

- **Will you have been studying** for hours by the time I arrive?
- **Will the children have been playing** in the park for two hours by evening?
- **Will the sermons have been influencing** people's thoughts for decades?
- **Will the clouds have been covering** the sky since morning?
- **Will pollution have been affecting** people's health for years?
- **Will winter have been bringing** snowfall for the past few weeks?
- **Will the guests have been waiting** for dinner for an hour by the time we reach?
- **Will the old buildings have been deteriorating** due to lack of maintenance for decades?

जॉय दो घंटे से अपने दोस्तों के साथ क्रिकेट खेल रहा होगा जब उसकी माँ उसे दोपहर के खाने के लिए बुलाएगी। वह तेज धूप के बावजूद खेल का आनंद ले रहा होगा। उसके दोस्त उसके लिए जयकार कर रहे होंगे जब वह रन बना रहा होगा। इस बीच, उसका छोटा भाई बालकनी से उन्हें खेलते हुए देख रहा होगा। जब तक खेल समाप्त होगा, लगातार दौड़ने के कारण जॉय बहुत अधिक पसीना बहा रहा होगा। उसकी माँ उसके लिए स्वादिष्ट भोजन लेकर इंतजार कर रही होगी।

अंत में, अपने दोस्तों के साथ शानदार समय बिताने के बाद वह थका हुआ लेकिन खुश महसूस कर रहा होगा।

Joy will have been playing cricket with his friends for two hours when his mother calls him for lunch. He will have been enjoying the game despite the scorching sun. His friends will have been cheering for him as he scores runs. Meanwhile, his younger brother will have been watching them play from the balcony. By the time the game ends, Joy will have been sweating heavily due to constant running. His mother will have been waiting for him with a delicious meal. Finally, he will have been feeling exhausted but happy after spending a great time with his friends.

What you and your friends will have been doing for a month after the final exam?

जॉय चिड़ियाघर में जानवरों को देखकर आश्चर्यचकित महसूस कर रहा होगा। बंदर एक शाखा से दूसरी शाखा पर मस्ती से कूद रहे होंगे। शेर अपने बाड़े में आराम कर रहे होंगे। पक्षी सुबह से मधुर स्वर में चहचहा रहे होंगे। आगंतुक उत्साह से घूम रहे होंगे। चिड़ियाघर के कर्मचारी जानवरों को ध्यानपूर्वक खिला रहे होंगे। बच्चे विभिन्न जीवों को देखकर आनंद ले रहे होंगे। हाथी खुद पर पानी छिड़क रहे होंगे।

will have been feeling, jumping, resting, chirping, walking, feeding, enjoying, spraying

Joy will have been feeling amazed to see the animals in the zoo. The monkeys will have been jumping from one branch to another playfully. The lions will have been resting in their enclosure. The birds will have been chirping melodiously since morning. The visitors will have been walking around excitedly. The zookeepers will have been feeding the animals with care. The children will have been enjoying their time watching different creatures. The elephants will have been spraying water on themselves.

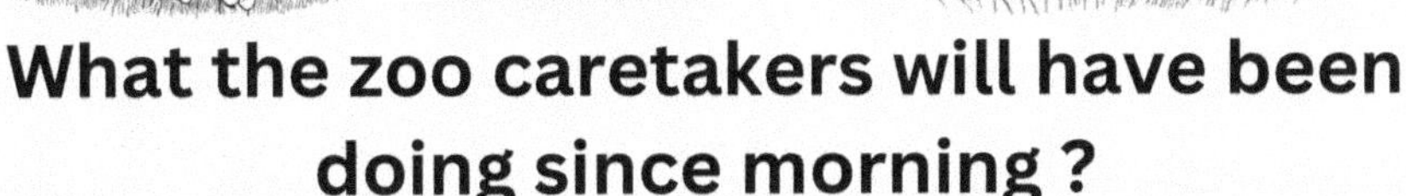

What the zoo caretakers will have been doing since morning ?

जॉय कुछ दिनों से वसंत ऋतु का आनंद ले रहा होगा। प्रकृति अपनी पूर्ण सुंदरता में होगी, जहाँ पेड़ नई पत्तियों से लदे हुए होंगे। पक्षी सुबह से मधुर स्वर में चहचहा रहे होंगे। ठंडी हवा सभी के मन को तरोताजा कर रही होगी। फूल चारों ओर अपनी खुशबू बिखेर रहे होंगे। साफ आसमान में सूरज चमक रहा होगा। सब कुछ, कुछ दिनों से वसंत का मनमोहक दृश्य बना रहा होगा।

will have been enjoying, chirping, refreshing, spreading, shining, creating

Joy will have been enjoying the spring season for a few days. Nature will have been in its full bloom with trees laden with new leaves. Birds will have been chirping melodiously since morning. The cool breeze will have been refreshing everyone's mind. Flowers will have been spreading their fragrance all around. The sun will have been shining brightly in the clear sky. Everything will have been creating a mesmerizing scene of spring for a couple of days.

Which is your favourite season of the year? Why?

जॉय एक साल से विभिन्न प्रकार के पत्तों का संग्रह कर रहा होगा और अब तक वह कई वनस्पति उद्यानों का दौरा कर चुका होगा। वह विभिन्न प्रजातियों पर शोध कर रहा है और उनकी अनूठी विशेषताओं को नोट कर रहा है। इस परियोजना के अंत तक, वह देश भर से दुर्लभ पत्तों को एकत्र कर चुका होगा। उसकी समर्पण भावना दूसरों को प्रेरित करेगी और जल्द ही, वह वनस्पति चमत्कारों पर एक पुस्तक प्रकाशित कर सकता है।

Making, visited, researching, gathered, will inspire, might publish

Speak English - 34

Joy will have been making a collection of a variety of leaves for a year, and he will have visited

many botanical gardens by now. He has been researching different species and noting their unique characteristics. By the end of this project, he will have gathered rare leaves from across the country. His dedication will inspire others and soon, he might publish a book on botanical wonders.

प्रकाशक विभिन्न शैलियों पर पुस्तकें एक महीने से प्रकाशित कर रहे होंगे क्योंकि वर्ल्ड बुक फेयर जल्द ही आयोजित होने वाला है। लेखक अपनी कृतियाँ लगातार प्रस्तुत कर रहे होंगे, इस आशा में कि

उनकी रचनाएँ संभावित पाठकों तक पहुँचेंगी। कहानी लेखक अपनी लेखन परियोजनाएँ पूरी कर चुके होंगे और अपने कार्य को अंतिम रूप दे रहे होंगे। इस बीच, प्रकाशक वितरकों से संपर्क कर रहे हैं ताकि उनकी पुस्तकों की पहुँच बढ़ाई जा सके। पाठक नई सोच और अनूठी कहानियों का उत्सुकता से इंतजार कर रहे हैं।

Speak English - 35

The publisher will have been publishing books on different genres for a month as the World Book Fair is going to be organized soon. The writer will have been submitting their publications all this while, hoping that their creations will reach potential readers. The story writers will have finished their writing projects and will be giving final shape to their work. Meanwhile, publishers are contacting distributors to expand the reach of their books. Readers are eagerly waiting to explore fresh ideas and unique storytelling in the upcoming fair.

अगले महीने तक, अंतरिक्ष यात्री छह महीने से अंतरिक्ष में यात्रा कर रहे होंगे, एक नए ग्रह पर उतरने की तैयारी करते हुए। वे उसके

वातावरण का अध्ययन कर रहे होंगे, यह सुनिश्चित करने के लिए कि यह मानव जीवन के लिए सुरक्षित है। उनका अंतरिक्ष यान तापमान, गुरुत्वाकर्षण और संभावित जल स्रोतों पर डेटा एकत्र कर चुका होगा। जैसे ही वे सतह पर कदम रखेंगे, उन्हें खोज की रोमांचक अनुभूति होगी। उन्होंने देखा होगा कि इस ग्रह के पेड़ रात में एक नरम, रंगीन चमक बिखेर रहे होंगे, जिससे एक जादुई जंगल बन रहा होगा और नदियाँ ज़मीन पर बहने के बजाय हवा में तैर रही होंगी, कांच जैसी झिलमिलाती हुई।

Traveling, preparing, studying, ensuring, collected, step onto, feel, noticed, emitting, creating, floating

By next month, astronauts will have been traveling through space for six months, preparing to land on a new planet. They will have been studying its atmosphere, ensuring it is safe for human survival. Their spacecraft will have collected data on temperature, gravity, and possible water sources. As they step onto the surface, they will feel the thrill of discovery. They will have noticed that the planet's trees will have been emitting a soft, colorful glow at night, creating a magical forest and the rivers instead of flowing on the ground, will have been floating mid-air, shimmering like liquid glass.

इंजीनियर सालों से पानी के नीचे शहर का निर्माण कर रहे होंगे, जिससे इसे परिवारों के रहने के लिए तैयार किया जा सके।

उन्नत गुम्बद महासागर के दबाव को सहने के लिए डिज़ाइन किए गए होंगे, जिससे एक सुरक्षित और आरामदायक आवास बनेगा। पारदर्शी सुरंगें लोगों को समुद्री जीवों के बीच चलने की अनुमति देंगी। वैज्ञानिक सूर्य के प्रकाश की नकल करने के लिए विशेष रोशनी विकसित कर रहे होंगे। समुद्र तल पर खड़े होने के बजाय, तैरते हुए घर समुद्र की सतह पर मंडरा रहे होंगे। वैज्ञानिक डॉल्फ़िन को मनुष्यों से संवाद करने के लिए प्रशिक्षित कर रहे होंगे। सड़कें रात में लोगों का मार्गदर्शन करने के लिए विभिन्न रंगों में चमक रही होंगी।

Constructing, making, designed, creating, allow, developing, hovering, training, glowing

Engineers will have been constructing the underwater city for years, making it ready for families to live in. Advanced domes will have been designed to withstand ocean pressure, creating a safe and comfortable habitat. Transparent tunnels will allow people to walk among sea creatures. Scientists will have been developing special lights to mimic sunlight. The floating homes will have been hovering in water instead of standing on the ocean bed. Scientists will have been training dolphins to communicate with humans. Streets will have been glowing in different colors to guide people at night.

What futuristic features can you imagine in an underwater city?

साल के अंत तक, Time-travelling बस छात्रों को अलग-अलग युगों में ले जा चुकी होगी। उन्होंने राजाओं और रानियों के भव्य महलों में घूमते हुए, रोमांचक युद्ध देखते हुए और प्राचीन सभ्यताओं को खोजते हुए समय बिताया होगा। इतिहास उनकी आँखों के सामने जीवंत हो उठा होगा, जिससे सीखना मज़ेदार और रोमांचक बन गया होगा। लेकिन भविष्य और भी ज़्यादा रोमांचक होगा! उन्होंने ऐसे जादुई मास्क देखे होंगे जो कुछ ही सेकंड में चेहरा बदल सकते हैं, जिससे लोग जब चाहें अपनी पहचान बदल सकें। सड़कों पर उड़ते हुए लोग दिखे होंगे, जो खास पंखों की मदद से आसमान में उड़ रहे होंगे, जिससे कारों की ज़रूरत ही नहीं रही होगी। दुनिया अजीब लेकिन शानदार हो चुकी होगी, और छात्रों ने जाना होगा कि भविष्य कितना अद्भुत हो सकता है!

Take, walk, watch, explore, come, seen, fill, use, make, show

Speak English - 38

By the end of the year, the time-traveling bus will have taken students to different eras. They will have walked through the grand palaces of kings and queens, watched fierce battles and explored ancient civilizations. History will have come alive before their eyes, making learning thrilling and real. But the future will have been even more exciting! They will have seen people wearing magic masks that change faces in seconds, helping them look different whenever they want. Streets will have been filled with flying people using special wings, making cars a thing of the past. The world will have been full of surprises, showing students how incredible the future can be!

Would you prefer to visit the past or the future in the time-traveling bus? Why?

भविष्य में मानव जीवन में अनेक परिवर्तन होंगे। विज्ञान और तकनीक इतनी प्रगति कर चुके होंगे कि लोग कल्पना भी नहीं कर सकते। लोग हवा में उड़ने वाली कारों का उपयोग करेंगे और घरों में रोबोट काम करेंगे। चिकित्सा क्षेत्र में इतनी तरक्की होगी कि कई असाध्य रोगों का इलाज संभव हो जाएगा। शिक्षा और कामकाज पूरी तरह डिजिटल हो जाएगा। लोग अपने घरों से ही काम करेंगे और स्कूलों की जगह वर्चुअल क्लासरूम होंगे। कृत्रिम बुद्धिमत्ता इंसानों की जिंदगी आसान बना देगी, लेकिन अगर सावधानी न बरती गई तो "आग से खेलना" भी साबित हो सकता है। पर्यावरण की स्थिति भी बदलेगी। अगर आज के लोग "ओखली में सिर डालेंगे," तो भविष्य में प्राकृतिक आपदाओं का सामना करना पड़ेगा।

will undergo, will have advanced, will use, work, progressed, become, replace, make, prove, put, face

Human life will undergo many changes in the future. Science and technology will have advanced so much that people will not even be able to imagine it. People will use flying cars, and robots will work in their homes. The medical field will have progressed to such an extent that the treatment of many incurable diseases will become possible. Education and work will be entirely digital. People will work from their homes, and virtual classrooms will replace traditional schools. Artificial Intelligence will make human life easier, but if caution is not exercised, it may prove to be like "playing with fire." The state of the environment will also change. If people today "put their heads in the mortar," they will have to face natural disasters in the future.

भविष्य में पारिवारिक संबंधों में बहुत बदलाव आएगा। तकनीक सभी को जोड़े रखेगी, लेकिन दिलों में दूरियाँ बढ़ सकती हैं। वीडियो कॉल पारिवारिक मेल-जोल की जगह ले लेंगे और घरेलू कामकाज रोबोट संभाल सकते हैं। संयुक्त परिवार दुर्लभ हो जाएंगे, और छोटे परिवार आम हो जाएंगे। यदि लोग रिश्तों को नजरअंदाज करेंगे, तो यह "जिम्मेदारी से हाथ धोने" जैसा होगा। लेकिन जो "परिवार के पेड़ को हरा-भरा रखेंगे," वे पीढ़ियों तक प्यार और अपनापन का आनंद लेंगे।

Change, keep, may grow apart, will replace, may handle, will become, ignore, keep, will enjoy

Family relationships will change a lot in coming time. Technology will keep everyone connected but hearts may grow apart. Video calls will replace family gatherings and robots may handle household work. Joint families will become rare and small families will be common. If people ignore relationships, it will be like washing hands of responsibility. But those who keep the family tree green will enjoy love and togetherness for generations.

How your family be placed in coming ten years?

Joy वर्ष 2035 तक अपने जीवन में अच्छी तरह बस चुका होगा। उसकी कड़ी मेहनत और समर्पण रंग ला 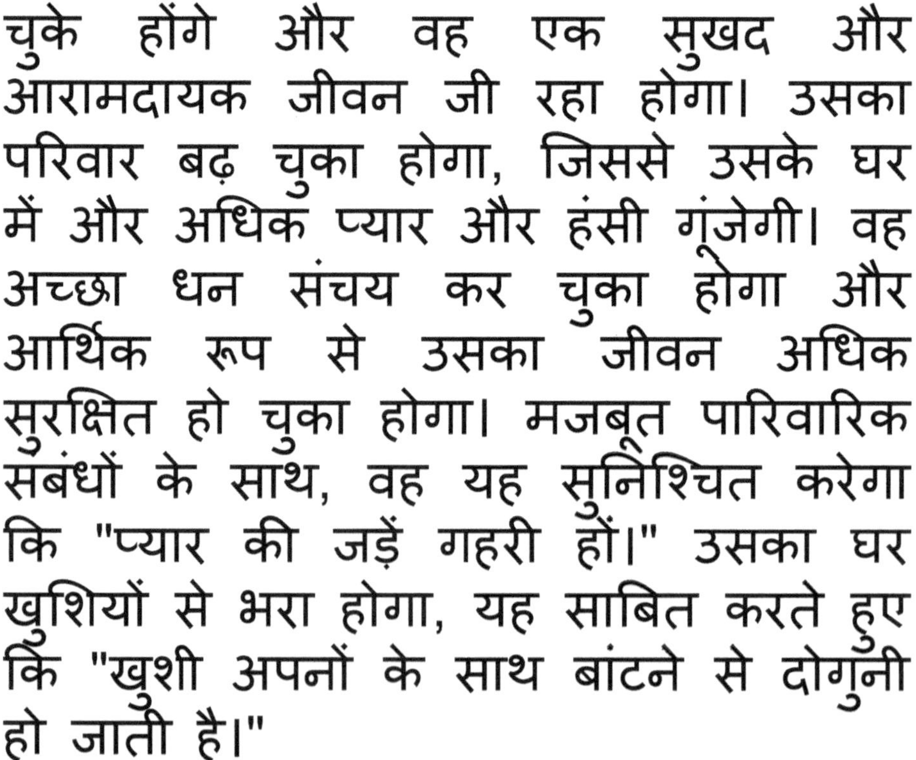 चुके होंगे और वह एक सुखद और आरामदायक जीवन जी रहा होगा। उसका परिवार बढ़ चुका होगा, जिससे उसके घर में और अधिक प्यार और हंसी गूंजेगी। वह अच्छा धन संचय कर चुका होगा और आर्थिक रूप से उसका जीवन अधिक सुरक्षित हो चुका होगा। मजबूत पारिवारिक संबंधों के साथ, वह यह सुनिश्चित करेगा कि "प्यार की जड़ें गहरी हों।" उसका घर खुशियों से भरा होगा, यह साबित करते हुए कि "खुशी अपनों के साथ बांटने से दोगुनी हो जाती है।"

will have settled, borne, living, grown, accumulated, gone, ensure, filled, doubles

Joy will have settled well in his life by the year 2035. His hard work and dedication will have borne fruit and he will be living a comfortable and happy life. His family will have grown, bringing more love and laughter into his home. He will have accumulated good wealth and financially his life would have gone more secure. With strong family bonds, he will ensure that the roots of love run deep.

His home will be filled with joy, proving that happiness doubles when shared with loved ones.

Where do you see yourself in coming ten years?

खुशी हमेशा बड़ी उपलब्धियों में नहीं होती। जब मैं बचपन में पतंग उड़ाता था, तो मेरी खुशी का ठिकाना न रहता। अब, जब कोई बच्चा मुस्कुराता है, तो मेरा दिल खुशी से भर जाता है। अगर हम छोटी-छोटी बातों में आनंद लेना सीख लें, तो जीवन सरल हो जाता है। जो लोग छोटी खुशियों को अनदेखा करते हैं, वे बड़े सुखों से भी वंचित रह जाते हैं। आखिरकार, खुशी एक अहसास है, जो हमारे नजरिए पर निर्भर करता है। एक बच्चा कागज की नाव से भी उतना ही खुश होता है जितना कोई महंगी कार से। उसे बारिश की बूँदों में नाचना अच्छा लगता है, मिठाई का एक टुकड़ा भी उत्सव जैसा लगता है। अगर हम आशीर्वादों से भरा जीवन जीना चाहते हैं, तो हमें बच्चों की तरह निश्चल और सरल होना होगा, जहाँ हर छोटी चीज में जादू दिखाई दे।

Found, used to fly, knew, smiles, fills, learn, becomes, ignore, deprived of, depends, finds, does, excites, feels, want to live, must be, feels

Happiness is not always found in big achievements. When I used to fly kites in my childhood, my joy knew no bounds. Now, when a child smiles, my heart fills with happiness. If we learn to enjoy the little things, life becomes simpler. Those who ignore small joys are deprived of greater happiness. After all, happiness is a feeling that depends on our perspective. A child finds as much joy in a paper boat as someone does in an expensive car. Dancing in the rain excites them and even a piece of candy feels like a celebration. If we want to live a life full of blessings, we must be as innocent and simple as a child, where every little thing feels magical.

Talk about the five things that bring smile on your face.

ज़िंदगी ने मुझे सिखाया है कि मंज़िल से ज़्यादा सफर की अहमियत होती है। जब मैं अपनी परीक्षाओं की तैयारी कर रहा था, तब महसूस हुआ कि संघर्ष, देर रात तक की पढ़ाई और छोटी-छोटी सफलताएँ मुझे उस अंतिम परिणाम से कहीं ज़्यादा मजबूत बना रही थीं। कल जब मैं अपने सपने पूरे करूँगा, तो पीछे मुड़कर इन्हीं कठिनाइयों को याद करूँगा और मुस्कुराऊँगा। अगर हम सिर्फ मंज़िल की नहीं, बल्कि सफर की खूबसूरती को भी महसूस करें, तो ज़िंदगी एक दौड़ नहीं, बल्कि एक खूबसूरत यात्रा बन जाएगी।

Speak English - 43

Life has taught me that the journey holds more value than the destination. When I was preparing for my exams, I realized that  the struggle, the late-night studies, and the small victories shaped me more than the final result. Tomorrow, when I achieve my dreams, I will look back and cherish the hardships. If we enjoy the ride rather than just waiting for the finish line, life will always be a road worth traveling, not just a race to win.

Write Five sentences on life.

एक दिन, दो जिद्दी बकरियाँ एक संकरे पुल के विपरीत सिरों पर पहुँचेंगी, जो एक तेज़ बहती नदी के ऊपर होगा। पुल इतना

संकरा होगा कि दोनों एक साथ पार नहीं कर सकेंगी, लेकिन कोई भी झुकने को तैयार नहीं होगी, क्योंकि दोनों अपने रास्ते का हकदार मानेंगी। उनका गुस्सा भड़क उठेगा और जल्द ही वे आपस में सींग फँसा लेंगी, एक-दूसरे को धक्का देकर हावी होने की कोशिश करेंगी। पुल उनका भार सहन नहीं कर पाएगा और चरमराने लगेगा, जब तक कि एक अंतिम धक्के के साथ वे संतुलन खोकर उग्र नदी में नहीं गिर जाएँगी। धारा उनके अहंकार को भी अपने साथ डुबोते हुए, उन्हें बहा ले जाएगी।

One day, two stubborn goats will reach opposite ends of a narrow bridge over a fast-flowing river. The bridge will be too narrow for both to cross at once but neither will yield, each believing they have the right of way. Their tempers will flare and soon, they will lock horns, shoving and struggling for dominance. The bridge will creak under their weight until, with a final push, both will lose balance and plunge into the raging river. The current will sweep them away, drowning their pride with them.

Stubbornness and pride lead to downfall, while wisdom and compromise pave the way to success.

जॉय बचपन में बहुत शरारती था। वह रोज़ दोस्तों के साथ खेलता था और नई-नई शरारतें करता था। अब वह बड़ा हो गया है और पढ़ाई पर ध्यान देता है। हर दिन वह स्कूल जाता है, मन लगाकर पढ़ता है और अच्छे अंक लाने की कोशिश करता है। अब तक, वह एक विज्ञान प्रतियोगिता जीत चुका है और अपने स्कूल की फुटबॉल टीम का कप्तान बन चुका है। आने वाले सालों में, वह एक सफल इंजीनियर बनेगा और अपने माता-पिता का सपना पूरा करेगा। अगले कुछ वर्षों में, वह एक प्रतिष्ठित विश्वविद्यालय से स्नातक हो चुका होगा और एक अच्छी नौकरी हासिल कर चुका होगा। वह कड़ी मेहनत करेगा और अपने जीवन में नई ऊँचाइयों तक पहुँचेगा।

Mischievous, childhood, pranks, sincerely, competition, successful, dream, prestigious, heights

Speak English - 45

Joy was very mischievous in his childhood. He used to play with his friends every day and come up with new pranks. Now, he has grown up and focuses on his studies. Every day, he goes to school, studies sincerely, and tries to score good marks. So far, he has won a science competition and has become the captain of his school's football team. In the coming years, he will become a successful engineer and fulfill his parents' dream. Within the next few years, he will have graduated from a prestigious university and will have secured a good job. He will work hard and reach new heights in his life.

जैसिका हमेशा से एक अच्छी गायिका बनना चाहती थी। बचपन में, वह हर दिन घंटों अभ्यास करती थी और स्कूल के संगीत कार्यक्रमों में भाग लेती थी। अब, वह एक

प्रसिद्ध संगीत अकादमी में प्रशिक्षण ले रही है और विभिन्न प्रतियोगिताओं में भाग ले रही है। अब तक, वह एक राष्ट्रीय स्तर की गायन प्रतियोगिता जीत चुकी है और एक संगीत एल्बम रिकॉर्ड कर चुकी है। आने वाले वर्षों में, वह एक प्रसिद्ध पार्श्व गायिका बनेगी और अपनी पहचान बनाएगी। कुछ वर्षों में, वह बड़े संगीतकारों के साथ काम कर चुकी होगी और अपने संगीत करियर में नई ऊँचाइयों को छू चुकी होगी।

wanted, used to do, used to take part, is taking, is participating, has won, has recorded, will become, will establish, will have worked, will have reached

अर्जुन हमेशा से एक सफल क्रिकेटर बनना चाहता था। बचपन में, वह हर सुबह क्रिकेट खेलता था और स्थानीय टूर्नामेंटों में भाग लेता था। अब, वह एक प्रतिष्ठित क्रिकेट अकादमी में प्रशिक्षण ले रहा है और राज्य स्तरीय मैच खेल रहा है। अब तक, वह एक अंडर-19 टूर्नामेंट जीत चुका है और अपनी टीम का उप-कप्तान बन चुका है। आने वाले वर्षों में, वह राष्ट्रीय टीम का हिस्सा बनेगा और

अंतरराष्ट्रीय स्तर पर अपनी पहचान बनाएगा। कुछ वर्षों में, वह कई रिकॉर्ड तोड़ चुका होगा और क्रिकेट जगत में एक महान खिलाड़ी के रूप में जाना जाएगा।

wanted, used to do, used to take part, is training, improving, has won, has become, , will become, will break, will be known

पुस्तकें हमेशा से ज्ञान का सबसे अच्छा स्रोत रही हैं। प्राचीन समय में, विद्वानों ने हस्तलिखित ग्रंथों को पढ़ा था और अपने ज्ञान का विस्तार किया था।

अब तक, लाखों किताबें प्रकाशित हो चुकी हैं, जिन्होंने अनगिनत लोगों को प्रेरित किया है। डिजिटल युग में, ई-बुक्स और ऑडियोबुक्स ने पढ़ने के तरीके बदल दिए हैं। आने वाले वर्षों में, किताबें और अधिक उन्नत हो चुकी होंगी और तकनीक के साथ जुड़ चुकी होंगी। वे न केवल मनोरंजन बल्कि शिक्षा का भी प्रमुख साधन बन चुकी होंगी।

read, had expanded, have been published, have inspired, have changed, will have advanced, will have integrated, will have become

मनुष्य ने हमेशा से अंतरिक्ष को समझने की कोशिश की है। वैज्ञानिकों ने कई शोध किए हैं और चंद्रमा पर कदम रख चुके

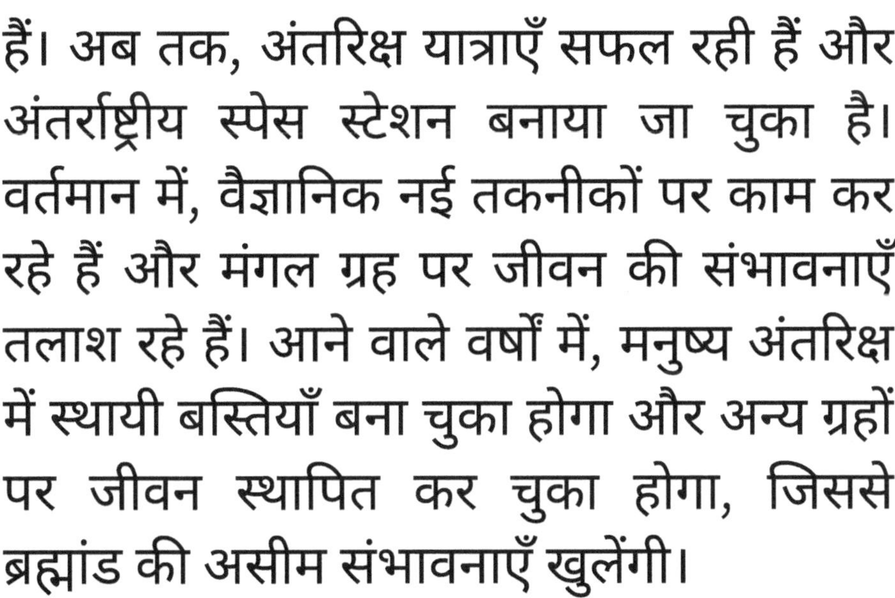

हैं। अब तक, अंतरिक्ष यात्राएँ सफल रही हैं और अंतर्राष्ट्रीय स्पेस स्टेशन बनाया जा चुका है। वर्तमान में, वैज्ञानिक नई तकनीकों पर काम कर रहे हैं और मंगल ग्रह पर जीवन की संभावनाएँ तलाश रहे हैं। आने वाले वर्षों में, मनुष्य अंतरिक्ष में स्थायी बस्तियाँ बना चुका होगा और अन्य ग्रहों पर जीवन स्थापित कर चुका होगा, जिससे ब्रह्मांड की असीम संभावनाएँ खुलेंगी।

Try to understand, made, stepped on, have been successful, has been made, working on new, looking for possibilities, will have constructed, will have got settled, will open

अब तक, दुनिया कई भयंकर युद्ध झेल चुकी है, जिन्होंने लाखों लोगों की जान ली है और देशों को तबाह कर दिया है। पहले विश्व युद्ध के समाप्त होने से पहले, कई राष्ट्र विनाशकारी संघर्षों में उलझ चुके थे।

दूसरे विश्व युद्ध की समाप्ति तक, दुनिया परमाणु हथियारों के खतरों को समझ चुकी थी। अगर देशों ने शांति के प्रयास नहीं किए, तो आने वाले वर्षों में, दुनिया और भी खतरनाक युद्धों का सामना कर चुकी होगी, जिससे मानवता को अपार क्षति पहुँचेगी।

has endured, have taken, have ended, had suffered, faced, had understood, will have witnessed, will have devastated

- How long will Joy have been reading this book by the time his parents return home?
- Will Joy have been gardening for an hour before lunch is ready?
- What food will Joy have been cooking when the guests arrive?
- How long will Joy have been feeding the birds by the time it gets dark?

Tell what professional activities people will have been doing for years

- How long will the boy have been working as a doctor by the end of the year?
- Will the boy have been cooking in the kitchen for more than two hours?
- How many months will the boy have been practicing as a construction worker before joining the new project?
- Will the boy have been doing the office job since his school holidays started?

- How long will the girl have been studying by the window by the time her exam starts?
- How many hours will the jogger have been running in the park by sunset?
- How long will the children have been playing soccer when their coach arrives?

- Why will the shopkeeper have been working all day without a break?
- Why will the teacher have been teaching at the same school for so many years?
- Why will the fishermen have been pulling in the net for so long despite the weather?

- How long will the students have been waiting in line before buying Tenses Are My Teacher?
- Will the teacher have been recommending this book to students throughout the fair?
- How many students will have been reading the book by the end of the event?
- For how long will the visitors have been browsing the stalls when the book caught their attention?
- Will the children have been discussing the grammar tips from the book with their friends all day?

Practice Answering The Questions

- How long will you have been living in this house by next January?
- Why will she have been cooking in the kitchen since early morning?
- What will they have been discussing for such a long time in the meeting?
- How long will we have been waiting for the plumber to arrive?
- Where will you have been working for the past five years?
- Why will he have been skipping breakfast every day for a month?
- How long will your parents have been planning this trip by the time you leave?
- What will your brother have been doing on the computer for hours?
- Why will the maid have been cleaning the same room again and again?
- How long will the kids have been watching TV when their dad returns home?

- How long will she have been driving to work when the new metro line opens?
- Why will the gardener have been watering the plants since morning?
- What will you have been reading for so many days?
- Where will they have been staying during the summer holidays?
- How long will you have been attending yoga classes by December?
- Why will the shopkeepers have been keeping their shops open so late?
- Who will have been helping grandma with her chores every weekend?
- What will your friend have been learning from that online course?
- How long will the dog have been barking when you return home?
- Why will she have been ignoring your messages all day?

- How long will the chef have been preparing meals when the guests arrive?
- Why will the student have been skipping his online classes all week?
- What will you have been doing at the library for so many hours?
- How long will the electrician have been fixing the wires by the time the lights come on?
- Where will your parents have been shopping while you were waiting at home?
- How long will the kids have been doing homework when the power goes out?
- Why will the neighbors have been complaining about the noise since morning?
- What will your sister have been searching for in the cupboard for so long?
- How long will the driver have been waiting outside your building?
- Why will the office staff have been working overtime this whole week?

1. My mother will have been knitting a sweater for two days by Sunday.
2. Ravi and I will have been running every morning for three weeks by then.
3. The teacher will have been checking papers for hours before the staff meeting.
4. Anita's cousins will have been staying at our place for a month by next weekend.
5. This machine will have been operating continuously for ten hours by noon.
6. Our neighbours will have been renovating their house for two months.
7. The little girl will have been waiting for the ice cream truck since afternoon.
8. A farmer will have been ploughing the field since early morning.
9. Joy's friends will have been playing cricket for hours before it starts raining.
10. My grandparents will have been living in that village for twenty years by next year.

Negative Sentences for Loud Reading

1. My sister will not have been learning French for very long.
2. The children will not have been playing in the park all afternoon.
3. The driver will not have been waiting at the station for an hour.
4. The baby will not have been sleeping through the noise.
5. The workers will not have been repairing the road since morning.
6. The scientist will not have been conducting experiments for months.
7. Ravi will not have been jogging every morning this summer.
8. The students will not have been attending the special classes regularly.
9. Her uncle will not have been visiting them frequently.
10. The singer will not have been performing for three hours by the time we reach.

Interrogative Sentences for Loud Reading

1. Will you have been studying for five hours by the time the exam starts?
2. Will she have been working at the hospital for ten years next month?
3. Will they have been living in this city for a decade by 2026?
4. Will he have been driving the whole night before reaching the destination?
5. Will I have been teaching this class for six months by the end of this term?
6. Will we have been waiting here for more than an hour before the bus arrives?
7. Will the children have been playing outside when the rain starts?
8. Will the machine have been running continuously for 24 hours by tomorrow morning?
9. Will your brother have been preparing for the interview all week?
10. Will Riya and Neha have been learning French for three years by next summer?

- मैं हर सुबह योग करता हूँ क्योंकि इससे मन शांत रहता है।
- वह स्कूल जाती है और रास्ते में पक्षियों को दाना देती है।
- बच्चे पार्क में खेलते हैं, लेकिन आज बारिश हो रही है।
- वह किताबें पढ़ना पसंद करता है और अब एक नई किताब पढ़ रहा है।
- मैं अंग्रेज़ी सीख रहा हूँ ताकि विदेश जाकर पढ़ाई कर सकूँ।
- वह जब भी खाली होता है, गिटार बजाता है।
- आज वह बहुत खुश है क्योंकि उसे उसकी मनपसंद नौकरी मिल गई है।
- हम रोज़ अभ्यास करते हैं, इसलिए हमारी टीम जीत रही है।
- तुम अक्सर देर से आते हो, क्या आज समय पर आओगे?
- वह अपने सपनों को पूरा करने के लिए दिन-रात मेहनत कर रहा है।
- मैं अब तक पाँच कहानियाँ लिख चुका हूँ – और भी लिखनी हैं।
- वह हमेशा सच्चाई बोलता है, इसलिए सब उसे पसंद करते हैं।
- मैं इस समय क्लास ले रहा हूँ, बाद में बात करता हूँ।
- तुम रोज़ जिम जाते हो – क्या अब तक कुछ फर्क पड़ा है?
- मेरी बहन नृत्य सीख रही है और अगले महीने मंच पर प्रस्तुति देगी।

- जब मैं छोटा था, मैं हर रविवार को पतंग उड़ाया करता था।

- वह अभी गाना गा रही है – सुनो कितना सुरीला है!

- हम कल नई फिल्म देखने जाएंगे, तुम भी चलो।

- उसने कल मुझे फोन नहीं किया, जबकि उसने वादा किया था।

- मैं दो घंटे से तुम्हारा इंतज़ार कर रहा हूँ।

- अगर बारिश हुई होती, तो हम पिकनिक पर नहीं जाते।

- बच्चे सुबह से शोर मचा रहे हैं – क्या तुमने कुछ कहा?

- वह अगले साल तक पेरिस में तीन साल से रह रहा होगा।

- जैसे ही ट्रेन आई, लोग भागते हुए चढ़ गए।

- क्या तुमने कभी पहाड़ों पर सूर्योदय देखा है?

- अगर तुम मेहनत करोगे, तो एक दिन जरूर सफल होगे।

- मैं खाना खा चुका हूँ, अब मीठा लाओ।

- वे पिछले हफ्ते गोवा घूमने गए थे।

- क्या वह कल तक अपना प्रोजेक्ट पूरा कर चुका होगा?

- वह अक्सर कहता है कि सपने देखो और उन्हें सच करो।

- वह रोज दूध पीता है लेकिन कल वह दूध नहीं पी पाया।
- वे स्कूल जाते हैं लेकिन पिछली रविवार को नहीं गए।
- हम हर शनिवार फिल्म देखते हैं, पर पिछले हफ्ते नहीं देखी।
- वह रोज सुबह टहलता है, पर कल बारिश हो रही थी तो नहीं गया।
- मैं अभी पढ़ाई कर रहा हूँ और शाम को मैं क्रिकेट खेलूँगा।
- वह अभी खाना बना रही है और रात को मेहमानों को खिलाएगी।
- वे गाना गा रहे हैं और थोड़ी देर में वे नृत्य भी करेंगे।
- हम अभी सफर कर रहे हैं और कल हम होटल में रुकेंगे।
- जब वह पढ़ रहा था, तब तक मैं अपना काम पूरा कर चुका होऊँगा।
- जब वे टीवी देख रहे थे, तब तक माँ खाना बना चुकी होंगी।
- जब हम स्कूल जा रहे थे, तब तक अध्यापक कक्षा शुरू कर चुके होंगे।
- जब वह रो रही थी, तब तक उसकी सहेली वहाँ पहुँच चुकी होगी।

- वह रोज स्कूल जाता है, लेकिन कल नहीं गया।
- हम हमेशा समय पर आते हैं, पर उस दिन हम देर से पहुँचे।
- मैं अभी किताब पढ़ रहा हूँ, बाद में फ़िल्म देखूँगा।
- वे अभी खाना बना रही हैं, शाम को मेहमानों को परोसेंगी।
- जब तुम पहुँचोगे, तब तक मैं खाना खा चुका होऊँगा।
- वे निकल चुके होंगे जब तक हम स्टेशन पहुँचेंगे।
- वह रोज गाना गाता है, और अगली बार भी गाएगा।
- मैं रोज़ सुबह दौड़ता हूँ, और कल भी दौड़ूँगा।
- वह अब मुझसे बात कर रहा है, लेकिन कल उसने कुछ नहीं कहा।
- हम अभी तैयारी कर रहे हैं, पर पिछली बार हमने कुछ नहीं किया था।
- उसने काम खत्म कर लिया था, अब वह आराम करता है।
- हमने पहले ही यात्रा की योजना बना ली थी, अब हम टिकट बुक करते हैं।

TENSE CHART

FUTURE

PRESENT

PAST

INDEFINITE

PAST
आ, ई, ए
2nd Verb
(-) did not + 1stv
(?) Did + Subject +
1stv ?

PRESENT
ता है, ती है, ते हैं।
1st verb form
(-) Do not / does not + 1stv
(?) Do/Does + Subject +
1stv
Use of 's' or 'es ' with verb
with he, she, it / single
subjects

FUTURE
गा, गी, गे।
Will/Shall + 1stv
(-) will/shall not + 1stv
(?) Will/Shall + subject + 1stv
Will/Shall : I & We

CONTINUOUS

PAST
रहा था रही थी रहे थे।
was/were + 1stv +
ing
(-) was/were + not +
1stv + ing
(?) Was/Were +
subject + 1stv + ing

PRESENT
रहा है। रही है। रहे है।
is, am, are + 1stv + ing
(-) is/am/are + not +
1stv + ing
(?) Is/Am/Are +
subject + 1stv

FUTURE
रहा होगा, रही होगी, रहे होगें।
will/shall + be + 1stv+ing
(-) will/shall not be
+1stv+ing
(?) Will/Shall + subject + be
+ 1stv+ing

PERFECT

PAST
चुका था, गया था, दिया था,
हुआ था, जीता था ।
had + 3rdv
(-) had not + 3rdv
(?) Had + subject +
3rdv

PRESENT
चुका है, गया है, दिया है, हुआ है
,जीता है।
Has/Have + 3rdv
(-) has/have + not + 3rdv
(?) Has/Have + subject +
3rdv
Has : He, She, It (Single
subjects)
Have : I, You & plural subjects

FUTURE
चुका होगा, गया होगा, दिया होगा,
हुआ होगा, जीता होगा।
will/shall + have + 3rdv
(-) will/shall + not have +
3rdv
(?) Will/Shall + subject + have
+ 3rdv

PERFECT CONTINUOUS

PAST
Time + रहा था, रही थी, रहे
थे।
had been + 1stv+ing
(-) had not been +
1stv+ing
(?) Had + subject +
been + 1stv+ing
Use of 'Since' or 'For'

PRESENT
Time + रहा है, रही है, रहे है।
has/have + been +
1stv+ing
(-) has/have + not +been
+ 1stv+ing
(?) has/have + subject +
been + 1stv+ing
Use of 'Since' or 'For'

FUTURE
Time + रहा होगा, रही होगी, रहे होगें।
will/shall + have been +
1stv+ing
(-) will/shall not have been +
1stv+ing
(?) Will/Shall + subject + have
been + 1stv+ing
Use of 'Since' or 'For'

Tenses Are My Teacher

Dear Reader,

I extend my heartfelt gratitude to you for completing the final volume — Volume 6 — of Tenses Are My Teacher. Your dedication to learning and the commitment you've shown throughout this journey is truly admirable.

This concluding volume not only focused on the Perfect Continuous Tenses but also provided ample practice from the earlier ones, allowing for meaningful revision and reinforcement. I sincerely hope that each page has supported you in speaking English more fluently and with greater confidence.

The positive response this series has received from readers like you has been both inspiring and deeply encouraging. Your trust in this work is something I cherish with immense humility.

Writing and composing these volumes has been a joyful and fulfilling journey for me. I took great care in arranging the content in a way that not only sharpens your speaking skills but also keeps you engaged and interested throughout. I'm truly happy to have accomplished this long-held dream and I firmly believe that these books will continue to serve as a dependable guide for English learners for years to come.

Thank you once again for your continuous support and more importantly, for the time and effort you've devoted to improving your language skills. I feel truly honored to be a part of your learning experience.

With best wishes,
AMRITASHAAN

प्रिय पाठक,

"Tenses Are My Teacher" की आखिरी कड़ी – वॉल्यूम 6 – को पूरा करने के लिए आपका दिल से धन्यवाद। आपने जिस मेहनत और लगन से इस पूरी सीरीज़ को पढ़ा है, वह सचमुच सराहनीय है।

इस अंतिम वॉल्यूम में जहाँ परफेक्ट कंटिन्युअस टेंस को समझाया गया है, वहीं पहले के वॉल्यूम्स की भी अच्छी तरह से दोहराई करवाई गई है, ताकि आपको बेहतर अभ्यास मिल सके। मुझे पूरी उम्मीद है कि इस किताब ने आपकी अंग्रेज़ी बोलने की क्षमता को और मजबूत किया होगा।

आप जैसे पाठकों से जो प्यार और सराहना मिली है, वह मेरे लिए बहुत हिम्मत बढ़ाने वाली रही है। आपने इस सीरीज़ पर जो भरोसा दिखाया है, उसके लिए मैं सच्चे मन से आभार प्रकट करती हूँ।

इन किताबों को लिखने और तैयार करने का सफर मेरे लिए बहुत ही खास और खुशी देने वाला रहा। मैंने हर बात का ध्यान रखा कि यह सामग्री आपकी अंग्रेज़ी सुधारने में मदद करे और पढ़ते समय भी आपको आनंद आए। आज जब यह सपना पूरा हुआ है, तो मुझे बेहद संतोष और गर्व महसूस हो रहा है। मुझे विश्वास है कि यह सीरीज़ आने वाले समय में भी सभी अंग्रेज़ी सीखने वालों के लिए एक उपयोगी साथी बनी रहेगी।

आपका साथ, आपका समय और आपका विश्वास मेरे लिए बहुत मायने रखता है। आप जैसे पाठकों की वजह से ही यह यात्रा इतनी सुंदर बनी है। मुझे खुशी है कि मैं आपकी सीखने की इस यात्रा का एक छोटा-सा हिस्सा बन सकी।

आपकी अपनी,
अमृताशान

Make Your Notes

Make Your Notes

Make Your Notes

Make Your Notes

Make Your Notes